PRIVACY-PRESERVING AI IN HEALTHCARE: TECHNIQUES AND APPLICATIONS

AJIT SAHU, SANJOY MUKHERJEE

notionpress
.com

INDIA • SINGAPORE • MALAYSIA

ISBN

Paperback 979-8-90560-351-8
Hardcase 979-8-90560-352-5

CONTENTS

6. Applications of Privacy-Preserving AI

7. Future Trends and Ethical Considerations

PREFACE

The rapid advancement of Artificial Intelligence (AI) has transformed the healthcare industry by enabling intelligent diagnosis, predictive analytics, personalized treatment, and efficient patient care. However, the increasing use of healthcare data has also raised serious concerns regarding privacy, security, and ethical handling of sensitive patient information. Protecting medical data while maintaining the effectiveness of AI systems has become one of the most important challenges in modern healthcare technologies.

This book, Privacy-Preserving AI in Healthcare: Techniques and Applications, aims to provide a comprehensive understanding of the methods, frameworks, and applications that ensure secure and privacy-aware AI solutions in healthcare environments. The book discusses key concepts such as data anonymization, federated learning, differential privacy, homomorphic encryption, secure multiparty computation, blockchain integration, and ethical AI practices. It also highlights real-world healthcare applications where privacy-preserving AI can enhance trust, compliance, and patient safety.

The purpose of this work is to bridge the gap between healthcare professionals, researchers, academicians, and students by presenting both theoretical foundations and practical insights into privacy-preserving technologies. We hope this book will serve as a valuable resource for individuals interested in the intersection of AI, cybersecurity, and healthcare innovation.

We express our sincere gratitude to all researchers, scholars, healthcare professionals, and technology experts whose contributions and studies have inspired this work. We also thank our families, colleagues, and well-wishers for their constant encouragement and support throughout the preparation of this book.

We hope that this book contributes to the development of secure, ethical, and trustworthy AI systems that can positively impact global healthcare.

DEDICATION

This book is dedicated to all healthcare professionals, researchers, educators, and innovators who tirelessly work toward improving human health and well-being through technology and scientific advancement.

We also dedicate this work to students and aspiring researchers whose curiosity and dedication continue to drive innovation in Artificial Intelligence and healthcare systems.

Above all, we dedicate this book to our families and loved ones for their unconditional support, encouragement, patience, and inspiration throughout this journey.

ACKNOWLEDGEMENT

The successful completion of this book would not have been possible without the guidance, encouragement, and support of many individuals and organizations.

We express our heartfelt gratitude to all researchers, academicians, and healthcare experts whose valuable studies and contributions in the fields of Artificial Intelligence, cybersecurity, and healthcare technology have provided the foundation for this work. Their pioneering efforts continue to inspire innovation in privacy-preserving healthcare systems.

We are sincerely thankful to our teachers, mentors, and colleagues for their continuous guidance, constructive suggestions, and encouragement during the development of this manuscript. Their knowledge and insights greatly enriched the quality of this book.

We would also like to acknowledge the support of our institutions, libraries, and online research platforms that provided access to valuable resources and references necessary for completing this work.

Finally, we extend our deepest appreciation to our families and friends for their patience, understanding, motivation, and unwavering support throughout the writing process. Their encouragement has been a constant source of strength and inspiration.

We hope this book will contribute meaningfully to research and advancements in secure and ethical AI-driven healthcare systems.

Chapter 1
INTRODUCTION TO PRIVACY IN HEALTHCARE AI

1.1 EVOLUTION OF AI IN HEALTHCARE

AI application in the medical field is not necessarily a new idea. The use of AI technology started to be applied in the early 1970s in order to address biological concerns and studies. Ever since, various artificial intelligence technologies have been developed to improve the healthcare industry by cutting costs, enhancing the quality of health, and ensuring efficient processes within the organization.

Before discussing the development of AI submissions in the healthcare area, it is important to define the concept of artificial intelligence. Artificial Intelligence, simply put, is defined as an application of computer science programs/models aimed at simulating human thoughts and performing cognitive processes like reasoning and problem-solving.

The AI products available in the current market come under the category of "Narrow AI." It implies that such a product is capable of performing some tasks better than a human being. Most of the current strategies involve methods of machine learning. Machine learning lets computers learn and work on their own (Nordlinger et al., 2020).

1.1.1. COMMON TYPES OF AI IN HEALTHCARE

These can be viewed as a point from which understanding begins, but one must recognize that there are many different interpretations of healthcare AI, and these concepts may mean different things to different individuals.

- **Machine Learning in Healthcare**

  Machine learning is one of the best-known implementations of artificial intelligence and uses pattern recognition to help a computer learn and then use its learning in comparable scenarios.

  Chatbots that help with scheduling, payments, or data organization in an imaging instrument, such as an MRI or CT scanner, are a few instances of machine learning in healthcare.

- **Deep Learning in Healthcare**

  Deep Learning, a higher form of machine learning that enables the machine to analyze the input data and make decisions based on them, like the ones we make with our brain, employs neural networks.

  Deep learning in medicine can be seen with such algorithms that benefit patients and their treatment by providing immediate alerts to clinicians.

- **Computer Vision (CV) in healthcare**

  The technique by which a computer learns from pictures and movies is another type of machine learning. Deep learning skills that can identify, analyze, and classify photos are present in certain sophisticated CV versions.

  The applications of CVs in healthcare comprise facial recognition and analysis of medical images.

- **Natural Language Processing (NLP) in healthcare**

  It is a form of machine learning that enables the computer to learn from human language and use the knowledge thus acquired to make decisions.

Examples of NLP in healthcare include the ability to use clinical notes to discover and notify doctors of patient follow-up possibilities.

- **Generative AI in Healthcare**

  This form of machine learning works on training different algorithms for writing programs, texts, images, and videos. The most famous application of such learning is ChatGPT created by Open AI. It has shown that it is fairly reliable at writing answers.

  Examples of generative AI in healthcare: While tools are still being developed, correspondence and documentation are potential use cases.

1.1.2. THE BENEFITS OF AI IN HEALTHCARE

AI can transform the healthcare industry through cost savings, greater accessibility to services, and improved quality of service delivery. All that is required is the implementation of AI within the organization.

The use of AI to assist healthcare providers in overcoming data and systems fragmentation, processing large data volumes, spotting trends, and making decisions rapidly to achieve better outcomes for patients represents one of the greatest advantages of AI within healthcare.

Finding the Right AI for Healthcare

Implementing any AI healthcare solution alone is insufficient. There are problems with point solutions, which address certain tasks independently. They require considerable investments in information technology in order to be maintained and are hard to scale up in various departments.

In the ability of AI to establish connections lies the power of AI in the healthcare industry. The concept of "connected intelligence system" operates like the central nervous system of hospitals through the integration of medical platforms and devices. By tackling both the medical and financial aspects, this approach brings immediate benefits.

AI and Healthcare: Doing More with Fewer Resources

Healthcare practitioners and health organizations can reap instant benefits from AI software that brings together diverse gadgets and applications.

Artificial Intelligence in Clinical Assistance

- Simplifying routine processes: Activities such as data entry, scheduling, and charting are examples of repetitive activities that could be streamlined using artificial intelligence.
- Lowering employee stress: Since artificial intelligence makes work more efficient by saving time on non-essential tasks, cognitive workload is significantly reduced.
- Enhancing diagnosis efficiency: Artificial intelligence facilitates quick and accurate decisions, hence promoting better judgment among healthcare practitioners.

Health System Optimization

Resource Allocation: AI can optimally allocate resources based on the needs of each patient encounter to address emerging situations.

Minimizing Operational Waste: Variability hampers efficiency. By making it possible to deliver high-quality care, AI enables efficient processes further down the line. Such as reducing readmission and hospital stays.

Quadruple Aim ROI

AI is capable of creating a domino effect ROI when used as a platform for the entire organization. Physicians and healthcare organizations utilizing AI could generate additional income streams based on clinically driven activities, including incidental findings and patient retention. However, the benefits do not end there.

The quadruple objective is a framework that prioritizes provider well-being, cost savings, population health, and patient experience. AI can directly help achieve this goal. AI in healthcare benefits both patients and providers by facilitating individualised care, raising illness awareness, and simplifying procedures.

1.1.3. IMPLEMENTING AI IN HEALTHCARE

Similar to the healthcare industry, there isn't a one-size-fits-all approach to clinical AI application. Three strategies have become popular, each with special benefits and difficulties.

- **Point solutions** might limit scalability and create data silos, but they can enable quick deployment and task-specific emphasis.
- Marketplaces allow the user to locate and select numerous AI applications in a centralized manner, but proficiency is required, as well as the potential inconsistency in systems and quality.
- Platforms help to centralize and scale up AI application implementation; they demand an upfront investment.

The main distinction between these different implementation methods exists in their approach to handling risks that arise from extensive technological changes. Healthcare systems need to conduct thorough assessments of data management challenges and infrastructure readiness and regulatory compliance and cybersecurity and workforce adaptation factors before choosing their AI vendor and deployment strategy.

1.1.4. THE ROLE OF AI IN THE FUTURE OF HEALTHCARE

AI technologies have been progressing like never before but still; the future holds much uncertainty. Nevertheless, some trends begin to emerge every year.

- **Emergence of Multimodal**

  Multimodal analysis and strong platforms are key components of AI's future in healthcare. The AI model will progressively incorporate the image with the patient's medical records through the use of EHR. This will allow doctors to focus on tougher issues by reducing the burdensome task of gathering data.

- **The Platform Imperative**

  Multimodal analysis is essential for AI models to function effectively. In the event that a patient is a non-smoker and does not have hypertension, the unintended discovery on the imaging test will not seem as significant. The use of AI can provide a more holistic perspective and enhance the quality of radiological reports.

- **Increased Governance**

  The role of governance is going to be much more important as artificial intelligence grows in its strength. To define how they plan to use these innovations and integrate them into their processes, hospitals and other health care institutions are creating AI Governance Committees. All of this is taking place at the same time as organizations like the "Office of the National Coordinator for Health Information Technology" (ONC) begin creating guidelines to manage the process.

1.2. IMPORTANCE OF DATA PRIVACY AND SECURITY

Data security and privacy have assumed greater importance in recent times due to the creation and transfer of large amounts of data. Data security can be defined as measures taken to ensure that there is no unauthorised access, theft, or any kind of damage caused to the electronic form of data. Privacy, on the other hand, ensures that personal information cannot be collected, processed, or shared without the individual's permission.

As a violation of either could result in serious repercussions, including loss of money, legal liability, reputation, and trust, it is important that data security and privacy be ensured.

In this section, the importance of data security and privacy is discussed in relation to individuals and organisations. section explores data security and privacy best practices, evaluates risks and consequences associated with data provides guidance on navigating the complex legislative landscape around data privacy (Salomon, 2012).

1.2.1. UNDERSTANDING THE DIFFERENCE BETWEEN DATA SECURITY AND DATA PRIVACY

However, while data security and data privacy are intended to serve distinct but complementary roles regarding the protection of data, at times these two terms tend to be used interchangeably.

Table 1.1: Difference Between Data Security and Data Privacy

Aspect	Data Security	Data Privacy
Focus	Defending data from attacks and unwanted access	Data management and responsible usage with regard to user rights
Objective	Prevent data breaches, theft, and loss	Verify user consent and data submission with privacy laws.
Methods	Encryption, firewalls, access controls	Policies for processing data, managing user consent, and agreement
Key Regulations	Often industry-specific (e.g., cybersecurity frameworks)	GDPR, CCPA, HIPAA
Role in Business	Protections from both internal and external threats	fosters faith by upholding and defending user data rights

A comparison of data security and data privacy is shown in Table 1.1, emphasizing the different goals, approaches, and functions of each in healthcare data management.

In other words, data security protects data from external threats, while data privacy guarantees that it is managed ethically and legally. Comprehending this disparity is essential as companies are gathering more and more personal information.

According to a recent Deloitte survey, 67% of consumers who use smartphones and 62% of consumers who use smart homes are worried about the security and protection of their personal data. This highlights the critical role that privacy and data security play in preserving client trust.

1.2.2. KEY PRINCIPLES OF DATA SECURITY AND PRIVACY

The concepts that help organizations ensure the protection of information and keep users' trust are the basis for successful implementation of measures of discretion, honor, and accessibility of information. The best-known example is the CIA Triad, created by:

- **Confidentiality:** Confidentiality helps in ensuring that any kind of sensitive data can only be accessed by authorized people. The process of protecting information from unauthorized disclosures is called confidentiality, which can be achieved through encryption and other forms of access controls.
- **Integrity:** Preserving the integrity of data at all times. Integrity of data makes sure that no changes are made to it while storing, processing, and transmitting it.
- **Availability:** Some of the examples of availability are disaster recovery, backups, and redundancy techniques.

1.2.3. DATA SECURITY STRATEGIES AND TECHNIQUES

To ensure adequate data protection, one needs to adopt multiple methods for minimizing the risks associated with data breaches. There are several techniques that may be used for effective data protection:

1. **Encryption:** Encrypted data cannot be understood by unauthorized personnel. Encryption is an essential measure that helps protect both transmitted and stored data from unauthorized persons since encrypted data becomes unreadable.
2. **Access Restrictions:** Access controls based on roles and responsibilities play a pivotal role in data protection since it

minimizes security risks. Role-based access control (RBAC) is a crucial data protection measure because it ensures that only those who have been authorized can access certain data.

3. **Firewall Security:** Firewalls act as the primary line of defense in protecting data against any external attacks. Firewalls monitor all the network traffic in order to regulate it in accordance with security protocols. This measure significantly reduces the risk of any external attacks as well as harmful communications.
4. **Multi-Factor Authentication:** Multi-factor authentication entails a requirement that two or more elements need to be authenticated before gaining access to the systems.
5. **Secure Network Security Protocols:** The "secure socket layer" (SSL) and "transport layer security" (TLS) are key network security protocols that help protect data during transmission.

1.2.4. DATA PRIVACY MANAGEMENT AND COMPLIANCE

Regulations adherence and proper data processing should be given topmost importance by organisations. For effective management of data privacy, transparency in data handling, clear guidelines and adherence to regulations should be put into consideration. Key aspects include:

- **Creation of Data Privacy Policy:** The organisations should create clear policies on how data should be collected, managed and stored. This way, both employees and customers will know what processes will be followed.
- **Conformity to User Consent:** Managing user consent is crucial in handling ethical use of data. Organisations should seek for explicit consent from their customers before collecting any data and ensure that it easy to change privacy settings.
- **Conforming to Regulations:** There are very high demands that are expected from GDPR, CCPA and HIPAA laws in regards to privacy of data. Failure to comply with the demands set could lead to dire results.

- **Data Subjects' Rights:** Users can view, correct and remove personal data from organisations as a outcome of several data privacy rules. It is important that organisations have systems for responding to such requests.

1.2.5. BEST PRACTICES FOR DATA SECURITY AND PRIVACY

Organizations can minimize risks, ensure compliance with regulations, and develop a culture that appreciates the importance of data security by implementing these best practices for data security. These include:

- **Regular Audits:** Audits of data security and privacy should be done regularly. The purpose is to be able to identify risks proactively and determine any vulnerabilities that may exist in the organization.
- **Update Software:** Any software concerning data security must be kept up-to-date. If there are new vulnerabilities or attacks, then the system will become more secure when it is updated.
- **Staff Training:** Human error is often one of the main risks that organizations face when dealing with data security.
- **Backup Data Security:** It is possible to prevent data loss caused by attacks on your business or due to some other problem with your network by maintaining secure backups. Encrypted backups and off-site backups are among the methods that can be considered best practices.
- **Access Control Measures:** You can leverage Multi-Factor Authentication (MFA) and Role-based access control to limit the use of your data to those who have the permission.

In summary, the implementation of best practices for data security and privacy is crucial in safeguarding sensitive information and building organizational trust. Some examples of best practices include regular audits, enhanced security systems, training employees, secure data backup measures, and strict access controls. Organizations can significantly decrease their cyber security risks through the implementation of best practices (Ouaissa & Ouaissa, 2024).

1.3. REGULATORY LANDSCAPE (HIPAA, GDPR, ETC.)

Over the past two decades, there has emerged a heavily regulated and dynamic healthcare industry due to various innovations in technology (such as cloud computing and telemedicine), changes in regulations, but, above all else, due to the urgent need to ensure the safety and privacy of patients.

Healthcare professionals must remain informed, be proactive, and utilize specialized technologies for regulatory obedience in order to navigate the complex regulatory environment effectively. This will allow them to maintain operational efficiency, ensure compliance, and ensure that they offer private treatment to their patients. In case of non-compliance, hefty fines and lawsuits may follow, along with damage to the reputations of large healthcare enterprises or small-scale clinics.

In the next section, the impact of AI on streamlining healthcare processes will be explored.

HIPAA

The most prevalent law in relation to healthcare in America is known as the "Health Insurance Portability and Accountability Act" (HIPAA), which was established in the year 1996. This law gives certain security measures concerning individuals' medical records as well as any other health-related information using uniform standards.

GDPR

The "General Data Protection Regulation" (GDPR) is an overarching data protection regulation that was enacted in 2018 by the European Union (EU). The core purpose of GDPR is to ensure that the legal environment is simplified for conducting business globally as well as improving data protection in terms of access to information for EU/EEA citizens.

HITECH

The HITECH (Health Information Technology for Economic and Clinical Health) Act was signed into law by President Obama in 2009 through the American Recovery and Reinvestment Act of 2009. Promotion of EHRs and other health IT technology is provided for within this law.

Five critical data privacy policies should be known by companies regardless of how many others there may seem to be:

1. **General Data Protection Regulation (GDPR)**

   The General Data Protection Regulation (GDPR) is one of the most significant data protection laws in the world. All EU members are subject to the GDPR, which was passed in 2018. Businesses that handle the personal information of EU individuals are subject to severe limitations under this rule.

   Eight essential provisions of the GDPR include:

   - The right to be informed – people have the right to know about the gathering, processing, storing, and erasure of their personal information.
   - The right of access – people can request a copy of their personal information.
   - The right to rectification – personal information can be corrected in case it is incomplete or incorrect.
   - Right to be forgotten: If someone asks for it, then his personal data should be erased.
   - Right to restriction of processing: A person may limit the processing of his personal data by a business organization. The above condition does not imply that a business organization cannot store personal data it has collected.
   - Right to data portability: People can access their personal data and use it at their will.
   - Right to objection: Individuals are capable of refusing the processing of their personal data at any time.

- Rights pertaining to automatic decision-making and profiling: Businesses are prohibited from utilizing the information gathered to profile people or make choices about them without considering people's opinions.
- Relevance: The GDPR applies to all companies that collect, process, and store data belonging to citizens of the European Union.

Yes, even non-EU citizens are considered when applying this legislation. Companies have to follow the GDPR requirements regarding data processing and information disclosure in order to stay compliant. Non-compliance is followed by penalties and huge fines.

2. **California Privacy Rights Act (CPRA)**

The California state statute that governs the protection of their residents' online privacy is referred to as the CPRA. The CPRA, which became active from January 1, 2023, mandates that all businesses review their processes for collecting, retaining, processing, and sharing data to ensure compliance with the statute. It started being enforced on July 1, 2023.

The "California Consumer Privacy Act" (CCPA), which came into effect on January 1, 2020, is an older act that the CPRA was formulated based on. The "California Privacy Protection Agency" (CPPA), a dedicated agency for protecting personal data information in the United States, will enforce the CPRA.

The Purpose of CPRA

The "General Data Protection Regulation" (GDPR), which went into effect in 2018, was created to ensure that any organization managing personal data acquired within the EU would be required to take proactive steps to protect both the data and the privacy of the data subjects. It applied to any company, whether or not it had its headquarters in the EU, that processed the personal data of data subjects who were inhabitants of the EU.

Similar in scope, the CPRA covers "for profit" organisations that handle the personal data of Californians that satisfy one of three requirements. For a business to be subject to CPRA jurisdiction, it must meet three requirements:

First, the CPRA will apply to companies that purchase, sell, or exchange the personal information (PI) of at least 100,000 customers or households. The CCPA's previous 50,000 customer thresholds has been updated to make it more flexible for small and medium-sized businesses (SMEs).

The California Privacy Rights Act requirements will also apply to businesses who generate $25 million in gross sales by January 1st of the year.

Lastly, CPRA also has authority over companies that get at least 50% of their total revenue from selling or distributing user personal information.

3. **Privacy & Electronic Communications Regulations (PECR)**

   PECR is a UK law that was approved in 2003 and is a forerunner of GDPR. The PECR establishes guidelines for electronic marketing, such as the following, whereas the GDPR controls the collection and use of personal data:

   - Marketing calls
   - Emails
   - Text messages
   - Cookies

   It also sets standards for secure correspondence and individual privacy with relation to billing, directory listings, and location information.

   Why it matters: PECR, which is regarded as a supplementary law to the GDPR, establishes rules for how businesses should promote to UK individuals. The regulation's governance for emails is one of its most significant requirements. The rule forbids companies from:

- Sending marketing emails to recipients without getting their consent beforehand
- Not providing an unsubscribe link in emails
- Keeping the "sent from" email address hidden
- Failure to comply with PECR may result in fines and other penalties, similar to the GDPR.

4. **Family Educational Rights and Privacy Act (FERPA)**

FERPA, a U.S. law, establishes data privacy requirements for student education records. All educational institutions that receive funds from the US Department of Education are subject to the law. A student has the following rights under FERPA:

- Examine and examine their educational records.
- Ask for any inaccurate information to be corrected.

Additionally, FERPA restricts who can access a student's data without prior authorization, including:

- School administrators with a genuine interest in education
- Other educational institutions to which a pupil is moving
- Officials designated for auditing or assessment
- Relevant parties in relation to a student's financial aid
- Organisations carrying out specific research for or on behalf of the institution
- Accrediting organizations

Why it matters: Destructions of FERPA may have far-reaching consequences. Student instruction records are more than simply an enhanced version of a report card. They frequently include identities, addresses, and other private information. Unless there is an emergency, FERPA protects students' educational information, even from their parents. Additionally, it gives students discretion over the usage of their educational records.

5. **Health Insurance Portability and Accountability Act (HIPAA)**

   What is HIPAA? Patient data privacy regulations were created by HIPAA, a comprehensive bill passed under the Clinton Administration in 1996. The law requires healthcare and health insurance businesses to protect patient information and data from theft and fraud. The regulation developed to impose restrictions on the safe transmission and maintenance of electronic healthcare records as times altered due to digitization.

   Why it matters: Fundamentally, HIPAA forbids any insurance company or healthcare provider from disclosing a patient's information without that patient's permission. This includes the possibility of data breaches; therefore, insurance companies and health organisations need to have a system in place to protect their networks. In a healthcare environment, HIPAA compliance also restricts who has access to a patient's records.

   Overall, the regulatory environment in relation to healthcare and information management has gained more prominence in recent years owing to the increasing adoption of electronic records, cloud computing technologies, and data-driven systems. Regulatory measures like the HIPAA, GDPR, HITECH, CPRA, PECR, and FERPA have played a vital role in safeguarding personal, educational, and healthcare information from misuse, data breach, and unauthorized access.

1.3.1. HIPAA COMPLIANCE IN HEALTHCARE DATA MANAGEMENT

In the current digital era, ensuring the security and privacy of sensitive data requires data management. The security of patient data is especially important in the healthcare industry. The HIPAA, which sets standards for protecting healthcare data, must be followed by all businesses that deal with patient information. the fundamental components of HIPAA compliance, the challenges associated with data management for compliance, and the steps that companies may take to achieve and maintain HIPAA compliance in their data management practices.

Understanding HIPAA Compliance

The necessity of complying with HIPAA regulations is necessary for the protection of patient data by health care firms. Besides protecting the rights of the patients, compliance with HIPAA will also help organizations in escaping any legal consequences as well as their reputation due to any data breach.

Key Components of HIPAA Compliance

Healthcare organisations must concentrate on a few essential elements in order to attain HIPAA compliance. Let's examine each of these crucial elements in more detail to better grasp their importance in attaining HIPAA compliance.

- **Data Privacy** – It is necessary for any healthcare organization to ensure that there is protection of patient information. One of the most important ways that patient information can be protected is through the use of encryption, which is the process whereby the data is converted into codes that can be deciphered using a particular key. Additionally, unauthorised individuals are prevented from accessing this sensitive data through restricted access, like the use of unique user names and passwords.
- **Data Security** – Security must be a top priority for any healthcare firm to avoid any form of breach. The use of firewalls and intrusion detection systems is some of the best ways of ensuring security because these will act as a shield to any potential attacker. Intrusion detection systems will monitor and correct any suspicious behaviour, while firewalls will monitor and control all traffic entering and leaving the network.
- **Administrative Safeguards** – In order to ensure that the healthcare workers have knowledge about HIPAA guidelines,

policies and training is very crucial. It is vital to formulate policies concerning use of patient information, conduct regular trainings about security and privacy guidelines, and impose penalties in case there is any non-compliance. The organizations can minimize their exposure to security threats by formulating appropriate administrative safeguards.

- **Physical Safeguards** – HIPAA compliance also involves the securing of the physical infrastructure in which patient information is stored. The unauthorised persons' access to such locations is restricted through security measures such as the use of key cards and biometric authentication. Through monitoring and recording the activities taking place at these locations, video surveillance systems provide added security. The physical documents that contain the patient information can be protected from being stolen or accessed inappropriately by storing them safely in places such as locked filing cabinets or rooms.
- **Technical Safeguards** – Healthcare organizations should apply the correct technology to protect the patient's personal health information because there is an increased use of electronic health records. Organizations will need to use secured servers, establish stringent authentication processes, and ensure that the data is encrypted during transmission. Other technologies include virtual private networks (VPNs) and secure emails, which are vital to ensure that data is transferred safely. Organizations will remain HIPAA compliant and prevent unauthorized access to patients' electronic health records by applying these technologies.
- **Documentation** – For an organization to demonstrate its adherence to the HIPAA regulations, the policies and processes must be appropriately documented. It is important for the organization to keep the documents of the risk assessment, training of employees, and policies on privacy and security. While the documentation serves as evidence of the compliance process during audits, it will serve as the way forward. The

healthcare organisations can demonstrate their commitment to the HIPAA regulation by maintaining documentation.

In summary, the implementation of HIPAA is a crucial aspect in the protection of patient health data. Putting administrative, technical, and physical measures in place can help guarantee that all healthcare data is protected and managed appropriately (AbuRumman, 2026).

1.3.2. STEPS TO ACHIEVE HIPAA COMPLIANCE IN DATA MANAGEMENT

Data management is critical to ensuring HIPAA compliance in today's digitalized healthcare industry. Given that healthcare providers deal with numerous confidential patient data, it becomes imperative to put in place appropriate measures that will guarantee data confidentiality, privacy, and protection against any data breach. HIPAA compliance demands thorough planning and monitoring to effectively manage risks.

- **Conducting A Risk Assessment**

  It is crucial that all to find potential risks and create mitigation plans, healthcare organisations carry out a comprehensive risk assessment before implementing the data management process. It is vital to analyze all the risks regarding the management of health care information.

  In order to achieve a good understanding of the possible risks associated with the employment of the data management process, it is vital to involve the key stakeholders of the organization at the stage of conducting the risk assessment. This collaborative approach can help to identify some of the areas that require attention, as well as address them through mitigation strategies.

- **Implementing A Data Management Plan**

  A detailed data management strategy is required to achieve HIPAA obedience. The data management strategy should encompass the collection, storage, access, distribution, retention, and destruction of data. Data auditing and quality management processes are also part of the data management strategy.

To strengthen the security of patient information, healthcare facilities should consider incorporating advanced technological means such as encryption, access restrictions, and data loss prevention solutions. By integrating these cutting-edge technological tools into the data management plan, Healthcare organisations can improve their data by integrating these cutting-edge technical tools into their data management strategy management procedures and minimize chances of data theft or unauthorized access to the information. The data management strategy needs to be reviewed and revised regularly.

Maintaining HIPAA Compliance in Data Management

- **Regular Auditing and Monitoring**

  Being HIPAA compliant requires auditing and monitoring activities continuously. Possible areas of vulnerability or non-compliance may be identified and sorted out before they become a problem by conducting audits and installing good monitoring tools. Data management systems will be assured to be HIPAA compliant through the processes described above.

- **Updating Policies and Procedures**

  The healthcare organizations should change their policies to meet the HIPAA guidelines due to advancements in technologies and changes in legal aspects. It is essential that data management policies be updated constantly due to evolving threats and changing circumstances.

- **Responding to Potential Compliance Issues**

  An organization must have an effective response plan in the event that any kind of compliance issue arises. This would consist of actions to be taken immediately upon discovery, notifications to be made both internally and externally, as well as measures that can mitigate the impact of the event. Organisations can lessen the effects of possible compliance concerns by responding quickly and using efficient remedial techniques.

HIPAA data compliance needs to be continuously ensured in order to secure patient data through good planning and implementation of effective data security measures. Healthcare organizations can protect themselves from any HIPAA compliance breach by conducting regular risk assessments, ensuring appropriate patient data handling techniques and procedures, proper policy formulation and compliance with regulatory requirements, and monitoring of data.

1.3.3. GDPR AND DATA PRIVACY REGULATIONS

Businesses must update their procedures and even reconsider their branding, services, and product designs in light of the GDPR, which altered privacy laws.

Consequently, even if the GDPR was passed in 2016, its core ideas are still applicable today. The core legal principles should direct every phase of a modern confidentiality program.

Recognize their goals and make sure your procedures for processing personal data align with them.

1. **Lawfulness, Fairness, and Transparency**

   Every time you handle personal information, you ought to have a good reason. The GDPR refers to this idea as lawfulness. Among the arguments in favour of data processing are:

   - You have permission from the user to do so.
   - To fulfil a contract, you have to perform it.
   - It's essential to complete a legal requirement.
   - To safeguard a natural person's vital interests
   - The task is carried out in the public interest.

- You can demonstrate that your legitimate interest is not superseded by the rights and interests of the data subject.

Lawfulness and fairness are closely related concepts under the GDPR. It suggests that you shouldn't purposefully hide information about what or why you are collecting data. To put it another way, people wouldn't be surprised if they found out how you were using their data. You must not misuse or mishandle the information you get in order to be fair.

Transparency and fairness go hand in hand. Being truthful, direct, and upfront with data subjects about who you are, why you are processing their personal information, and how is what is meant by transparency. If you follow it, you treat your data subjects fairly.

2. **Purpose Limitation**

   The GDPR's second principle limits the use of data for particular purposes. This purpose restriction ensures that data is only "collected for specified, explicit, and legitimate purposes" under the GDPR.

   There needs to be a clear objective for the data processing. They also need to be disclosed to individuals through a privacy notice. Finally, you have to follow them to the letter, processing data only for the purposes you have stated.

   If you want to use the data you have collected for a new purpose that is incompatible with your original purpose, you must specifically get consent again unless there is a clear legal necessity or function.

3. **Data minimization**

   Only obtain the data necessary to achieve your goals. The GDPR's concept of data minimization is this. For example, if you want to gather subscribers for your email newsletter, you should simply ask for the information needed to distribute the newsletters. Don't gather personal data that isn't relevant to your objective, such phone numbers or residential addresses.

4. **Accuracy**

   It is your duty to make sure the data you collect and store is accurate. Create checks and balances to correct, eliminate, or modify incoming data that is erroneous or incomplete. Plan regular audits to ensure that stored data is clean.

5. **Storage Restrictions**

   Establishing data retention periods is one of the best ways to adhere to the GDPR's storage limits policy. Set a deadline for anonymizing any data that isn't being used. One of the best ways to adhere to this storage limitation policy is to set data retention periods. Set a date for anonymizing any data that isn't in use.

6. **Integrity and Confidentiality**

   In summary, one should always protect the integrity and discretion of the data collected by ensuring that there are no external or internal threats to such data. In this regard, one should be prepared and be attentive beforehand to ensure that data is not accidentally lost, damaged, or destroyed.

7. **Accountability**

   The GDPR authorities are aware that a business may say it complies with all requirements without actually doing so. As a result, they want some level of accountability: You need to have the processes and paperwork in place to show that you follow the data processing requirements. Supervisory authorities may ask for this information at any time. In this case, documentation is crucial. It generates an audit trail that you and the authorities can use to demonstrate your accountability.

Under the GDPR, fairness and lawfulness are closely related concepts. It implies that you shouldn't purposefully hide information about what or why you are collecting data. Put another way, people wouldn't be surprised if they found out how you were using their data. You must not misuse the information you are given in order to be fair.

The seven GDPR guiding principles encapsulate the core and technique of best practices for data processing. The GDPR also specifies what data controllers and processors need to do in order to respect each of the tenets.

These seven principles guide all processing operations and business activities, from the design stage through the whole data processing lifecycle, rather than being a component of the operational jigsaw. The easiest way to achieve this is to implement privacy by design and default.

Visit our comprehensive guide to GDPR Compliance to discover more about the principles of the GDPR and how this operates. It serves as a guide for fully integrating the GDPR principles into your privacy program.

Who Needs to Be GDPR Compliant

You are legally obligated to abide by the GDPR if you handle PII of people in the UK and EU. If you don't, you risk paying steep fines of up to €20 million, or 4% of your global yearly income.

Processors, controllers, and organizational structures all have different GDPR implementation timelines, although they usually range from six to 36 weeks.

After implementation, companies must regularly execute an internal GDPR assessment to show that they are still in compliance. Additionally, a company may seek for an optional accreditation.

Differences Between HIPAA Vs. GDPR Compliance

HIPAA and GDPR are two key data privacy regulations that aim to safeguard private data. HIPAA regulates the protection of healthcare data in the US, whereas GDPR safeguards all forms of personal data of people living within the European Union.

In addition, there is a huge disparity in terms of individual rights offered by GDPR versus HIPAA. GDPR offers wide-ranging rights including access, correction, and even deleting personal data, while HIPAA mainly safeguards patients' medical records.

It can be stated, therefore, that while both HIPAA and GDPR help secure private data, the former relates specifically to health data, while the latter covers other sectors besides health.

Similarities Between HIPAA and GDPR Compliance

Organisations that adhere to HIPAA or GDPR already have data security protocols in place. HIPAA and other regulations differ more than they are similar. There is some framework overlap with GDPR:

- Both call for restricted access to private information.
- Both call for techniques to identify unauthorised PHI modifications.
- PHI encryption is necessary for both in transit and at rest.
- Both need a designated DPO.
- Both give businesses the protection they need to concentrate on their customers and patients. and the privacy of employees

In spite of the differences in scope, jurisdiction, and compliance requirements between HIPAA and GDPR, the primary goal of these two acts is the same, namely, the protection of sensitive data. By complying with HIPAA and GDPR, businesses can improve their data governance frameworks and protect their reputations (Sharma, 2019).

1.4. CHALLENGES IN HEALTHCARE DATA SHARING

The sharing of healthcare data is an integral part of today's healthcare system. The sharing of healthcare data requires many things that have to be done before data can be shared effectively. Issues such as ensuring patient privacy, security, and obedience with laws and procedures can be considered as some of the main concerns when sharing healthcare data. With the advancement in technology and the use of health informatics, the challenge associated with the sharing of healthcare data has increased immensely.

1.4.1. THE CHANGING CONSENT MANAGEMENT ENVIRONMENT

Digitization of medical records along with the growth of online healthcare services has greatly changed the way data is exchanged in healthcare. This process has posed many challenges related to the confidentiality and security of medical data. Proper management of consents does not only enhance privacy protection but also promotes trust within relationships between doctors and patients.

Healthcare organizations like yours face some of the following challenges in relation to the handling of consent:

- Fragmented consent between different processes and systems
- Data integrity throughout all steps of the healthcare process
- Challenges in implementing consent through multiple channels
- Great risks involved in confirming compliance with legal guidelines such as GDPR

The healthcare sector is currently making strides towards "computable consent," which allows computers to selectively share patient information according to privacy controls. The Privacy and Consent Workgroup of the Sequoia Project has been studying the existing systems, highlighting the importance of standards-driven automation that ensures the exchange of health information with privacy considerations.

Finding Balance Between Innovation and Privacy Protection

Wearable health technology, telemedicine, and AI-based diagnosis are just a few examples of how far medicine has advanced through the use of digital technologies. Nonetheless, as more data becomes vulnerable during transmission, the risks associated with security threats and cyberattacks have grown considerably, placing conflicting demands on innovation and security.

Consumers expect complete transparency regarding the use of personal data; as such, privacy must always come first in order to maintain the trust of consumers. This will require the creation of practices that are both ethical and technologically innovative (Pezoulas et al., 2020).

1.4.2. REGULATORY COMPLEXITIES DRIVING CHANGE

There have been stringent regulations put in place regarding data privacy in the field of health care. With technology advancing and healthcare services expanding in the digital world, it becomes imperative to ensure that all the patient data collected is in accordance with the set regulations.

- **Stricter Privacy Regulations**

  Wearable health technology, telemedicine, and AI-based diagnosis are just a few examples of how far medicine has advanced through the use of digital technologies. Nonetheless, as more data becomes vulnerable during transmission, the risks associated with security threats and cyberattacks have grown considerably, placing conflicting demands on innovation and security.

  Consumers expect complete transparency regarding the use of personal data; as such, privacy must always come first in order to maintain the trust of consumers. This will require the creation of practices that are both ethical and technologically innovative.

- **Navigating Multiple Regulatory Frameworks**

  There are a number of overlapping laws, each of which requires varied consent management approaches, that must be followed by your medical firm. Consequently, there is a lot of complexity involved, especially when you consider companies operating across several jurisdictions with varying privacy laws such as GDPR, CCPA, and HIPAA. It is challenging to develop standardized consent mechanisms due to conflicting legislative frameworks.

- **Regulatory Complexities Driving Change**

  There are increased healthcare data privacy laws and regulations in place, making compliance increasingly difficult for your company.

- **Increased Healthcare Data Privacy Laws**

  Within five years from now, all healthcare providers must conform to higher privacy standards, meaning there is need for strategic planning and infrastructure. In order to collect, process, and transfer personal data, current regulations, including GDPR, CCPA, and HIPAA, highlight the significance of obtaining "free, specific, informed, and unambiguous" consent.

  The above guidelines offer individuals some level of control over personal data, as well as accountability and transparency in the use of this personal information. Good consent management systems are not just an obligation for Healthcare institutions handling substantial volumes of personal health data, including genetic information, test results, and patient files.

- **Navigating Multiple Regulatory Frameworks**

  The healthcare firm will have to contend with multiple regulations that overlap with each other and have unique requirements with respect to managing consents. This creates a high degree of complexity, especially when the firm is operating in multiple jurisdictions that have different privacy laws such as HIPAA, CCPA, and GDPR. It is hard to develop standardized consent methods due to the disparity among various legal regimes.

  Regulatory issues have a major impact on how health care institutions handle patient information. In order to comply with privacy laws, good governance is necessary along with the management of data security. This will enhance the confidence of the patients.

1.4.3. TECHNICAL IMPLEMENTATION CHALLENGES

Putting in place consent management systems which would satisfy patient expectations and regulatory compliance brings about a range of technological issues for health care institutions.

- **Fragmentation of Consent Management Systems**

  According to research carried out in the sector, many health care organizations do not have a unified consent management process; thus, there is a possibility of data fragmentation which makes it difficult to utilize data without proper permission. It also becomes hard to keep updated information regarding the consent choices of patients.

- **Incorporation with Legacy Architecture**

  Health care institutions often have legacy architectures which were not built keeping in view the requirements of current consent management technologies. There are several issues involved in the integration of legacy architecture with current consent management technology, and huge investments might become necessary.

- **Complex Data Ecosystems**

  Given the transfer of data among multiple entities, ranging from providers to insurers and academics, to third-party services, the healthcare data ecosystem has become increasingly complex. Technical solutions of a sophisticated nature are required in order to be able to track consent preferences as data moves from one system to another within the network.

- **Data Prior to Consent**

  Regarding data collected prior to the implementation of the present-day consent regulations, your company likely has some specific challenges. From an ethical and technical standpoint, there are significant concerns regarding how to handle such legacy data in compliance with new standards while retaining its relevance for clinical and scientific purposes.

In rapid, implementation-related issues have a critical impact on the process of managing consent and data exchange in the health care industry. The problems associated with disjointed consent mechanisms, poor infrastructure, complicated data environments, and managing historic data all impede effective implementation. Solving these problems will be important not only for enhancing privacy and meeting regulatory requirements but also for ensuring the efficiency of the process itself.

1.4.4. PATIENT ENGAGEMENT AND UNDERSTANDING CHALLENGES

Understanding and engagement on the part of the patient play crucial roles in the successful management of healthcare consents. In a digitalized healthcare system, patients are supposed to give their consent for their personal data regarding health care matters to be collected, stored, and distributed. Yet, there are several problems that prevent the patient from fully comprehending what they need to consent to.

- **Comprehension Challenges**

  Perhaps, one of the largest obstacles to comprehension is patients' inability to understand technical terms used in legal documents such as consent forms and data usage policies. The language used is hard to comprehend and, therefore, patients might give their consent without realizing what exactly they agree to.

- **Issues with Voluntary Consent**

  Patients often have no choice but to give in to the terms of data sharing in order to be granted access to the healthcare facilities and/or the digital healthcare services. In view of the ever-growing incorporation of technological healthcare solutions into the system, patients can perceive consent for such procedures as obligatory rather than voluntary, thus undermining the moral principle of consent.

- **Dynamic Nature of Data Usage**

  The development and application of new forms of healthcare technologies as well as new methods for using patients' data proceed at a fast pace. Patient data, which has been used for some initial goal, may be applied for conducting research, analyzing data, developing artificial intelligence tools and other healthcare-related purposes. Such dynamics complicate the processes of obtaining consent from the patient.

- **Issues Related to Digital Literacy and Accessibility**

  One more issue that needs mentioning is the difference in digital literacy levels amongst patients. There is always a possibility that some patients, especially elderly patients and those coming from disadvantaged backgrounds, might have problems using digital healthcare management systems and obtaining consent on the internet. Poor availability of technologies and inability to work with technological tools might hinder the process of collecting healthcare-related information.

  To conclude, patient engagement and understanding can be viewed as key aspects affecting the performance of consent management systems within the framework of healthcare data management. Issues ranging from lack of comprehension and voluntary agreement, changes in the process of data utilization, to digital literacy problems might impact patient consent. Thus, hospitals need to focus on developing consent mechanisms that will be convenient for patients.

1.5. CHAPTER SUMMARY

In this chapter, emphasis was placed on the increased utilization of AI in the field of healthcare and its influence on the improvement of healthcare services, decision making, and efficiency. In this regard, the chapter detailed the development of AI in healthcare as well as major types of AI technology like ML, DL, CV, NLP, and Generative AI. Additionally, various advantages of AI technology in healthcare have been elaborated upon in this chapter, which included better diagnostics, automating processes, optimizing healthcare systems, and better healthcare delivery. Various ways of implementing AI technology in healthcare were also discussed, apart from discussing the future of AI technology in healthcare.

The concepts of data security and privacy were distinguished from each other, while confidentiality, integrity, and availability were discussed as key concepts in the context of information security. Threats to data security included cyber-attacks, unauthorized access, data breaches, and failure to comply with regulations. In addition, different security techniques were presented, such as encryption, access controls, firewalls, two-factor authentication, and network security protocols. The practices of conducting audits, training employees, updating software, and creating backups were listed as best practices.

Some of the key regulations in this regard are HIPAA, GDPR, HITECH, CPRA, PECR, and FERPA. Regulatory compliance is essential for ensuring the security of patients' data and adhering to ethical standards in managing health care data. HIPAA compliance requirements were discussed, along with how HIPAA compliance can be achieved, and the key principles of GDPR associated with data processing, consent, accountability, and data protection were highlighted.

The final part of the chapter examined problems in terms of data sharing and consent management in healthcare. Such problems as lack of uniform consent mechanisms, regulatory constraints, technical issues, patients' knowledge of their rights, and other aspects were identified. In summary, the chapter indicated that privacy and security of the data used by AI in healthcare is necessary.

Multiple Choice Questions (MCQs)

1. **Which factor primarily drove the evolution of AI in healthcare?**
   A. Increase in hospital staff
   B. Availability of large healthcare datasets
   C. Reduction in patient numbers
   D. Elimination of medical errors

2. **Early applications of AI in healthcare mainly focused on:**
   A. Robotics surgery
   B. Medical imaging and diagnostics
   C. Hospital management
   D. Patient counseling

3. **Why is data privacy critical in healthcare AI?**
   A. To increase hospital profits
   B. To ensure faster diagnoses
   C. To protect sensitive patient information
   D. To reduce the use of technology

4. **Which of the following is an example of sensitive healthcare data?**
   A. Weather reports
   B. Patient medical records
   C. Hospital building plans
   D. Public advertisements

5. **What does HIPAA primarily regulate?**
   - A. AI algorithms
   - B. Patient data privacy and security in the U.S.
   - C. Global internet usage
   - D. Medical equipment standards
6. **GDPR is a regulation associated with:**
   - A. India
   - B. United States
   - C. European Union
   - D. Australia
7. **One major challenge in healthcare data sharing is:**
   - A. Lack of doctors
   - B. Data standardization issues
   - C. Too much funding
   - D. Limited diseases
8. **Which of the following is a key concern when sharing healthcare data?**
   - A. Data redundancy
   - B. Patient confidentiality
   - C. Data color
   - D. File format
9. **AI systems in healthcare must comply with regulations to:**
   - A. Increase speed
   - B. Avoid ethical and legal issues
   - C. Reduce staff workload
   - D. Improve internet access

10. **What is a common risk of poor data security in healthcare AI?**
    A. Faster processing
    B. Data breaches
    C. Improved diagnostics
    D. Better communication

Answers

1	2	3	4	5	6	7	8	9	10
B	B	C	B	B	C	B	B	B	B

Chapter 2

FUNDAMENTALS OF PRIVACY-PRESERVING TECHNIQUES

2.1. DATA ANONYMIZATION AND DE-IDENTIFICATION

The process of concealing or removing any form of personally identifiable information (PII) from any given data set with the intention of ensuring that the identities of individuals linked with such data remain private is referred to as data anonymization.

Without impacting its functionality in software testing and analysis or other valid applications, anonymization involves making the identification of individuals based on data more challenging.

The purpose of data anonymization is to alter and conceal PII and sensitive data to ensure that it cannot easily be linked to an individual's identity. In other words, it reduces the chances of re-identification so as to enhance the security of such data.

The discovery of personal identifiers such as names, addresses, phone numbers, passports, or social security numbers is often the first step towards anonymization. To secure the data, the identifiers are concealed or altered using cryptography or noise.

Complete anonymity cannot be achieved using anonymized data because there exist ways through which one might re-identify individuals from their data. This is especially true when the anonymized data is combined with publicly available sources of data (El Emam, 2013).

2.1.1. HOW DATA ANONYMIZATION PROTECTS PERSONAL PRIVACY

Through reducing the chances of revealing and using people's private information, data anonymization becomes an important process for protecting the privacy of individuals. There is a greater likelihood of individuals' private data being accessible and used without their consent because there are larger volumes of data available and stored today.

A breach of trust for the client or consumer is more significant than a loss of security for the company when personal information is compromised. Numerous privacy issues, including as identity theft, discrimination, and contract violations, may result from such attacks.

Data anonymization significantly reduces the capacity of unauthorized users to access or utilize personal information by concealing or removing PII from datasets. Data anonymization helps organizations to comply with data privacy regulations, such as APPI, CPRA, DCIA, HIPAA, PDP, SOX, GDPR, and DORA European regulations, which require businesses to take preventative measures to protect an individual's confidential data, in addition to preventing privacy breaches and safeguarding individual rights. Importantly, data can still be used for analysis, business insights, research, and decision-making even after it has been anonymized, all without disclosing any personal information.

2.1.2. CORE TYPES OF DATA ANONYMIZATION

There are 6 core types of data anonymization, including:

1. **Data masking**

   Sensitive information, including credit card numbers, driver's license numbers, and Social Security numbers, is substituted by data masking software with either meaningless characters, numbers, or symbols or with fake but presumably real data. Test data can be made available for testing or development without jeopardizing the real information's privacy by masking it.

A number of methods, including character replacement, data shuffling, and truncation, can be used to apply data masking to individual fields or to entire datasets. On demand or in accordance with a schedule, data can be hidden. When there is not enough production data, the data masking suite includes synthetic data generation and data tokenization, which permanently replaces personal data with random placeholders.

2. **Pseudonymization**

   Through replacing personal identification details with pseudonyms or pseudonymous identifiers, pseudonymization achieves anonymity of the data. Personal names, address information, and Social Security numbers are just a few examples of personal data that gets replaced under this process.

   The use of pseudonymized data allows for the dataset to be employed for legitimate purposes without increasing the risks of exposing or misusing the PII. Unlike tokenization technology for data processing, pseudonymization can be reversed and often complements other privacy techniques, like data masking rather than encryption.

3. **Data aggregation**

   Data aggregation, which combines data from many different sources to provide a consolidated picture, is utilized for trend analysis, pattern recognition, or insights to make decisions. Data in text form, numbers, and categories can be aggregated in various levels of detail, from basic aggregations to complex calculations.

   There are several applications for aggregated data, including analysis, reporting, and visualization, among others, which can be presented in several forms. Additionally, it can be used on masked or anonymized data to protect the privacy of individuals.

4. **Random data generation**

   The process of random data generation may be applied to an entire dataset or individual rows or columns within a database, effectively mixing up the data in a random manner, thus obscuring valuable data.

   In order to ensure that the subjects participating in clinical trials are not only randomly selected but also randomly allocated to different groups within a study, the process of random data generation is often combined with data masking or data tokenization techniques.

5. **Data generalization**

   Data generalization is employed to conceal any PII, such as an individual's residence or age, from unauthorized users by replacing the actual value with a generalized one. Generalized values involve replacing individual values with a range, set, or geographic area.

   An example would be replacing the exact address 1705 Fifth Avenue with uptown, midtown, or downtown. Similarly, the age value of 55 could be applied to middle-aged individuals or those aged between 50 and 60 years.

6. **Data swapping**

   Data swapping substitutes fictional but comparable data values with actual data values. For example, a fictional name like Robbie Simons can be substituted for a genuine name like Don Johnson. Alternatively, a fictional address, such as 15 Parkside Lane, can be substituted for a real one, such as 186 South Street. Similar to the random data generator, data swapping substitutes new, fictional values for the original ones instead of shuffling the data.

   To conclude, various forms of data anonymization are crucial when it comes to ensuring that sensitive information is protected without compromising the use of such data for analysis and decision making. Data masking, pseudonymization, aggregation, generating random data, generalization, and data swapping are some of the common techniques used by companies to mitigate the risks associated with unauthorized access to and re-identification of their employees. Such techniques are extensively used in sectors such as healthcare and finance among others to ensure that data is kept private and confidential (Weber & Heinrich, 2012).

2.1.3. ADVANTAGES AND DISADVANTAGES OF DE-IDENTIFICATION AND DATA ANONYMIZATION

In determining whether to go for de-identification or anonymization for purposes of research in health care settings, there is always a need to strike a balance between confidentiality and data usability. Both de-identification and anonymization techniques have their strengths and weaknesses, which manifest themselves differently in terms of compliance, data usability, and operational considerations.

De-identification makes it possible to keep diverse clinical, demographic, and temporal data without necessarily incorporating any form of personal identification like names and social security numbers. This high degree of specificity is highly valuable for research initiatives such as outcome assessment studies, machine learning model training, and quality assurance projects which are dependent on patient-level analysis. De-identification may also facilitate the safe re-association of data with its original source for clinical follow-up or safety reasons, when required. The disadvantage of de-identification is that it is vulnerable to re-identification; it has been proven that using external datasets, one can identify the individual from the de-identified dataset [1]. Thus, even though de-identified data is no longer considered personal, data protection policies such as HIPAA and GDPR apply to de-identified data.

In contrast, anonymization emphasizes the permanent protection of privacy by making the data immune to strict regulatory frameworks such as GDPR. It makes data-sharing across borders, archiving, and open science more feasible, since there will be no need for continuous consent or compliance with data movement laws. Anonymization is applicable when creating public health dashboards, benchmark datasets in publications, and extensive collaboration efforts where individual-level monitoring is unnecessary. But the downside to this technique is the reduction in data fidelity; the generalization, aggregation, or addition of noise that comes with anonymization may conceal key insights in clinical patterns, rare event identification, and analytical bias. In the words of the International Association of Privacy Professionals, "de-identification is not anonymization (in virtually all cases)".

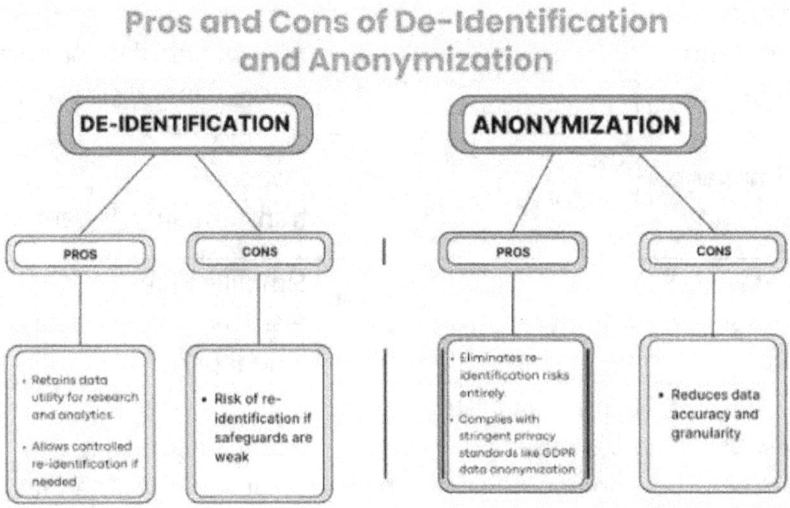

Figure 2.1: Pros and Cons of De-identification and Data Anonymization

Diagram 2.1 shows how de-identification and anonymization help protect sensitive information while ensuring data usability and compliance with privacy laws.

Here's a quick comparison of these two approaches:

Table 2.1: Comparison Between De-Identification and Anonymization

Aspect	De-Identification	Anonymization
Privacy protection	Moderate - re-identification is possible using quasi-identifiers and external datasets	Strong - individuals cannot be re-identified by reasonable means
Data utility	High - detailed clinical, temporal, and demographic data is preserved	Lower - data is aggregated or generalized, reducing detail
Regulatory status	Treated as protected personal data under HIPAA, GDPR, etc.	Falls outside data protection laws when truly irreversible
Re-linkage capability	Possible via secure keys for follow-up or validation	Not possible - transformation is permanent
Cross-border sharing	Requires compliance with transfer rules and adequacy assessments	Simplified - fewer restrictions when data is no longer personal
Best use cases	Longitudinal studies, AI/ML training, quality improvement, vendor risk analytics	Public datasets, open benchmarks, epidemiological studies, educational use

Table 2.1 compares de-identification and anonymization based on privacy protection, data utility, regulatory status, re-linkage capability, cross-border sharing, and common use cases.

To accomplish, both de-identification and anonymization are essential forms of techniques that can be used to protect confidential information related to healthcare and ensure its usability. While de-identification allows more flexible utilization of healthcare data in clinical research and artificial intelligence applications, it still entails a risk of de-identification, and regulatory requirements should be met.

Meanwhile, anonymization ensures better privacy since all personal identifiers will be irreversibly deleted, which, however, can decrease the accuracy of collected information. Hence, depending on specific needs, organizations should select one of the discussed approaches to data handling.

2.1.4. COMMON DATA ANONYMIZATION USES CASES

Here's a list of data anonymization use cases, broken down by industry sector:

1. **Healthcare**

   Data anonymization is used by the healthcare sector to safeguard patients' privacy while allowing their information to be utilized for authorized applications like analysis, reporting, and research. Data anonymization is used in the healthcare industry to protect treatment details, personal information, and medical histories.

   For instance, data anonymization could be used to find patterns in disease outbreaks or to assess the effectiveness of specific medication treatments without disclosing patient PHI (Protected Health Information).

   Additionally, it is utilized to adhere to data privacy regulations such the Health Insurance Portability and Accountability Act (HIPAA).

2. **Financial services**

   Data anonymization is used by financial services firms, including banks, brokerages, and insurance organisations, to safeguard private data, including transaction information, financial histories, and PII. Anonymized data can be shared and used by financial institutions for reporting, analysis, and research without jeopardizing the privacy of their clients.

   For example, data anonymization is used to test the efficacy of marketing campaigns or find fraud patterns without disclosing any personally identifiable information.

The US "Securities and Exchange Commission" (SEC), the Financial Industry Regulatory Authority (FINRA), and PCE DSS, which safeguards payment details, are just a few of the data privacy laws that financial institutions must abide by.

3. **Telecommunications**

   Data anonymization is employed by media and telecommunications companies to protect sensitive information, such as PII, call history and messages, and location data. There is no need to be concerned about compromising client privacy when sharing and analyzing anonymized data.

   For example, data anonymization can help enhance network performance, measure the effectiveness of marketing strategies, or detect patterns in usage without revealing any PII.

   Furthermore, it can be employed to comply with data protection regulations, like the rules established by the United States Federal Communications Commission (FCC), which offer privacy protections that provide broadband customers with safeguards, choices, and transparency with regard to their personal information.

4. **Government**

   The process of data anonymization is employed not only by the local authorities but also by the national authorities to protect confidential data, such as tax files, voting files, and citizen files.

   For instance, data anonymization may be employed to investigate the effectiveness of any public programmed, conduct research on populations, or find links between poverty or crimes.

   In addition to this, data anonymization may also be employed to comply with legislation governing personal data security, such as the California Privacy Rights Act (CPRA) and the General Data Protection Regulation (GDPR).

Finally, data anonymization has become one of the most necessary processes used by many businesses to protect sensitive and personal data while providing efficient possibilities for using data for analysis, research, reporting, and decision making. For instance, companies from the fields of healthcare, finance, telecommunications, government, etc. make use of data anonymization for protecting confidentiality and avoiding data breaches. Through the use of this process, data anonymization helps minimize risks related to unauthorized identification of personal data.

2.2. DIFFERENTIAL PRIVACY CONCEPTS

Privacy by Design (DP) provides a framework for a robust privacy paradigm, which brings the privacy challenge of analyzing data sets that contain personally identifiable information into the realm of mathematics. Simply put, differential privacy requires that the outcome of the analysis should remain unchanged even if an individual's data changes. This protects people from adversaries who attempt to discover personal information about them. It is examined in relation to the gathering, processing, and dissemination of aggregate statistics that range from machine learning to basic statistical estimations.

In today's connected world, gathering and evaluating aggregated data is crucial, but are you taking all the required precautions to protect the privacy of the people who provide it? Taking the appropriate security measures while handling customer data is not only morally and ethically right, but it's also required by law to stay in compliance and prevent large penalties, terrible publicity, and harm to your company's reputation.

Using the differential privacy concept is one increasingly popular and successful technique to stay out of trouble. Differential privacy is a characteristic of a data point or process that establishes whether or not that data can be deemed private, rather than a particular privacy approach like de-identification.

Differential privacy, to put it another way, is the mathematical definition of the level of protection, alteration, or anonymization required before data is sufficiently private to prevent re-identification with the person associated with it (Le Ny, 2020).

2.2.1. WHAT IS DIFFERENTIAL PRIVACY?

By characterizing the patterns of groups inside a dataset, Differential Privacy is a mathematical definition that offers a strict foundation for creating privacy-preserving technologies that enable organizations to share information about a dataset. All personal information about individuals is kept private, even while the patterns are shared. The idea is to successfully extract valuable information from a dataset while safeguarding the privacy of persons inside it.

Differential privacy is widely regarded as being better than other conventional de-identification and information concealment techniques because it guarantees verifiable, quantifiable privacy guarantees, protects against post-processing information leakage, and allows for the modular design of an analysis from simpler analyses. Some or all of these characteristics are absent from other methods.

In order to ensure statistical validity and protect the privacy of individuals in the data sets, researchers have recently created differentially private procedures and techniques that enable organisations to do data analysis on aggregated sensitive data. Differential privacy is not a cure-all, though, because when data is accessed by differentially private mechanisms on a regular basis, information leakage eventually builds up. Differential privacy is therefore not appropriate for every use case that calls for privacy. Specifically, for the transmission of extremely sensitive data, Differential Privacy cannot take the role of cryptographic techniques.

2.2.2. HOW DIFFERENTIAL PRIVACY WORKS

A randomized method, $\mathcal{M}$[D], is applied to any data that is exposed to an external observer from a dataset, D, in order to establish differential privacy. The method protects privacy by adding controlled randomness, or "noise," to the exposed data. A variety of methods, including shuffling, randomized response, and additive noise, can be used in a differential privacy mechanism. In essence, the specific mechanism chosen depends on the type and calibre of information the observer is looking for. The system is intended to provide information-theoretic privacy, meaning that whether or not data on a specific person is included, the results of a given analysis are essentially unchanged.

For instance, the analytical mechanism $\mathcal{M}$ on both datasets should yield a comparable result if you have Database D and subtract data on person X to generate Database D′:

$\mathcal{M}$[D]~$\mathcal{M}$[D′], in a way that makes it impossible for the observer (the data analyst viewing the mechanism›s output) to determine with enough certainty if any particular person was or was not retrieved from the data set. We can conclude that the analysis does not meet Differential Privacy requirements if the outcome is not roughly the same.

In Differential Privacy, the privacy parameter ε—also referred to as the privacy loss or privacy budget—is adjusted to determine the strength of the privacy assurance. Each person's dataset is given greater privacy when the privacy budget is lower. However, when ε is decreased, the system applies more noise or "randomness." The exposed information becomes useless for any practical use if the privacy budget is too tiny.

The quantification of data privacy loss caused by the mechanism, $\mathcal{M}$, is represented by the privacy budget. It can be demonstrated that this provides the three primary benefits of differential privacy:

- Measurable assurances of privacy
- Protection against post-processing data leaks, which prevents the extraction of new insights after processing
- Enables modular analysis design from more basic analyses

Building a "least noisy" technique that ensures privacy while maintaining utility is the primary difficulty.

Types of Differential Privacy

Systems for Differential Privacy must be practically designed with security and privacy in mind. While privacy refers to what can be deduced from a data release, security refers to who is permitted to view a piece of data. Each of the two main Differential Privacy deployment types targets a distinct threat model:

- Central Differential Privacy (CDP): In CDP, a trusted centralized data curator gathers and stores individual data in an unencrypted manner. The curator then applies Differential Privacy to the sensitive data, releasing the results to an untrusted data analyst. However, because it creates a single point of failure for data breaches and burdens the trusted curator with ethical and legal obligations to protect data privacy, this strategy is unsuitable for many applications.
- Local Differential Privacy (LDP): In LDP, each person uses a local Differential Privacy mechanism on their device to alter their own data at random. These random or noisy responses are used by the data analyst to deduce aggregate statistics of the combined data. As a result, LDP is thought to be more secure than CDP. However, LDP is far less effective than CDP since it requires adding a lot more random noise or perturbation to the data in order to achieve the same level of privacy. Therefore, compared to CDP, this method is typically more successful for considerably bigger datasets.

There are benefits and drawbacks to both the central and local models. Differential privacy can be used in conjunction with fully homomorphic encryption (FHE) to get around these flaws. Differentially private functions can be computed securely thanks to FHE, which permits computing on encrypted data without first decrypting it. This method eliminates the need for a reliable curator and combines the security advantages of the local model with the accuracy of the central model. The only enterprise-ready solution that can integrate several strategies and/or privacy-enhancing technologies (PETs) is the Duality Privacy Preserving Data Collaboration Platform.

2.2.3. BENEFITS OF DIFFERENTIAL DATA PRIVACY

Due to a few clear improvements over earlier data privacy strategies, differential data privacy is becoming more popular.

- **Presupposes Identifying Data**

  It can be challenging or even impossible to ask a human (or perhaps even a machine) to distinguish between identifying and non-identifying information. In differential privacy, the randomness value is determined by assuming that all information has identified potential.

- **Less Exposure to Privacy Attacks**

  Through linkage attacks, even de-identified data can be connected to the people it depicts. However, differential data privacy is a potent tool for protecting data since it is more resilient to attacks based on auxiliary information.

- **Security of Compositions**

  The combined information obtained from several separate analysis is one way that de-identified data may result in a loss of privacy. When the same data is subjected to two different studies, the combined data can offer sufficient information to connect the data to its sources.

  Differential data privacy, however, is compositional, thus the precise degree of privacy lost from conducting two private studies can be ascertained. With that knowledge, reasonable privacy assurance measures can be implemented.

- **Automatically Adjusts Query Result Accuracy**

  Differential privacy will automatically modify a query's correctness according on the query's characteristics. This helps guarantee that the outcomes you receive are as accurate as feasible while maintaining a respectable degree of privacy. The more precise and comprehensive the results, the less privacy risk a query pose.

- **Personalized Privacy Levels**

  There is no one-size-fits-all method since differential data offers a customized amount of privacy. This prevents some data from being overexposed to leaks or from being excessively obscured for meaningful analysis.

Concluding, differential privacy ensures high standards of privacy while still being able to do valuable data analysis and research. Thanks to its ability to minimize privacy risks, prevent information leakages, and provide flexible privacy standards, it has been recognized as an efficient and trustworthy solution for secure storage of sensitive data.

2.2.4. CHALLENGES OF DIFFERENTIAL PRIVACY

Even with proper implementation, differential privacy is not perfect. For starters, it doesn't cover every possible cybersecurity issue. When differential privacy is applied to a data point, individual level analysis is no longer feasible. This prevents an analyst from discovering personal information about a particular person, which is excellent for preventing hackers but not so good for using data for customized analysis.

Another challenge is determining the appropriate level of distortion or noise required to maintain privacy. Nevertheless, as the concept of differential privacy gains more popularity, there should eventually be some agreement reached regarding the ideal level of ε — at least, in the context of certain use cases (Cheng, 2022).

2.2.5. DIFFERENTIAL DATA PRIVACY USE CASES

In relation to use cases, the following are some of the most recent and noteworthy ways that differential data privacy has been made public:

- In 2014, Google unveiled Randomized Aggregable Privacy-Preserving Ordinal Response, or RAPPOR, a differential privacy technique. It is a feature of the Chrome browser that enables Google to examine and extract significant insights from the use of its flagship browser without permitting sensitive data to be traced or accessed without authorization. Google took things a step further in 2019 with the release of open-source differential privacy libraries.

- Differential data privacy is employed in Apple-designed and released iOS and macOS devices, enabling the security and analysis of personal data from search searches and health information to the most often used emojis.
- In the 2020 Census, the U.S. Census Bureau used differentiated privacy for the first time, enabling it to gather comprehensive data on the demographics of American people without permitting the tracking of that data.

In summary, differential privacy has emerged as a valuable tool for ensuring data privacy by enabling large companies and government entities to gather and analyze data without revealing personal identifiers. The practical implementation of this concept in various technological and governmental sectors highlights its efficiency in balancing data utility and robust privacy safeguards.

2.3. CRYPTOGRAPHIC FOUNDATIONS FOR DATA PROTECTION

A crucial component of contemporary cybersecurity, cryptographic security safeguards everything from remote access to digital payments. In this article, we break down the core components of cryptography, how it's used in practice, and why effective key management is essential for maintaining trust, compliance, and resilience

What Is Cryptographic Security?

Cryptographic security refers to the use of mathematical techniques — encryption, hashing, and digital signatures — to protect information and ensure that data can only be accessed or changed by those who are authorized. Email verification, financial transactions, secure login procedures, and data integrity are all made possible by it.

NIST defines cryptographic security as "the security achieved by the appropriate implementation of a technically sound cryptosystem". A cryptosystem refers to an assortment of methods used for encoding and decoding confidential data.

There are three primary objectives that are at the heart of cryptographic security:

- Confidentiality: Preventing unauthorized access.
- Integrity: Ensuring data hasn't been altered.
- Authentication: Verifying the source of information.

When data is stored, transmitted, or accessed, cryptographic mechanisms work behind the scenes to ensure only official parties can access or modify information (Goldreich, 2001).

2.3.1. WHY IS CRYPTOGRAPHIC SECURITY IMPORTANT?

Modern-day enterprises rely on cryptographic security not only for protecting their confidential information but also for maintaining their credibility. Cryptographic technology ensures the secure transactions required by today's financial institutions, cloud computing services, e-ID verification systems, and software integrity checks.

The following are some of the numerous factors making cryptographic methods highly significant:

- **Digital Integrity:** No matter whether you are dealing with ecommerce sites or citizen data within government agencies, cryptography techniques, including encryption and digital signatures, will help to keep your valuable data safe from any possible modifications during transfer or storage.
- **Cost Reduction:** Lack of proper security for cryptographic assets, such as keys or digital certificates, can cause serious data breaches, regulatory penalties, and even downtime. The average cost of data breach globally is estimated at $4.9 million. Cybercrime involving identity theft also can cause fraud issues resulting in $7 million losses per year.
- **Access Control:** Cryptography helps to provide controlled access to various digital services utilized by customers, citizens, and employees alike on a daily basis.

- **Regulatory Compliance:** Many regulations require implementing advanced cryptographic protection for personal data, online transactions, and IT infrastructure, failure to comply with which can result in audit failures, fines, and even exclusion from the market.
- **Ensuring Customer Relationships:** The consumers and stakeholders have expectations about data privacy and security. This is where the need for encryption arises; it helps not only reduce risks related to security but also strengthens the resolve to ensure privacy and security.

In summary, cryptographic security enables the processes and experiences that characterize today's businesses. Those that prioritize its implementation will have a competitive advantage over their counterparts that view it as nothing more than a mere compliance issue. Symmetric Encryption vs. Asymmetric Encryption

Among the core aspects of cryptography is the use of encryption. It refers to converting information from a readable form into an unreadable form so as to ensure that the information remains confidential. Encryption does this by limiting access to decryption.

The two major types of encryptions include:

1. Symmetric encryption utilizes the same key for both encryption and decryption of data. It is highly efficient and well-suited for the task of encryption of vast amounts of data.
2. Asymmetric encryption, also referred to as public key encryption, makes use of two keys – one private and the other public. Asymmetric encryption plays an important role in enabling key exchange and digital signatures, and is essential for TLS and PKI technologies.

Cryptography is the core component of any modern, digitally oriented era, where there is a need for secure transmission of information and its proper storage within organizations and online websites. Using encryption methods, digital signatures, and secure access control policies, organizations can achieve the safe management of their information, maintain trust of their customers, and ensure compliance with all necessary legal requirements.

2.3.2. COMPONENTS OF CRYPTOGRAPHIC SECURITY

Cryptographic security is not a single technique; rather, it is a system of interacting technologies used to secure sensitive information, authenticate identities, and build trust. Cryptographic techniques can be categorized into several broad groups:

Cryptographic Algorithms

The algorithms behind cryptography are math used to provide the security in question. The algorithms serve the purpose of performing operations such as data encryption and hashing. Algorithms include:

- **Advanced Encryption Standard (AES):** AES is the symmetric cryptographic algorithm used to encrypt data at rest. The algorithm encrypts information in fixed-size blocks by using one secret key. This makes AES an appropriate method of protecting large amounts of data, for example, databases.
- **Elliptic Curve Cryptography (ECC):** ECC is an asymmetric cryptographic algorithm which provides effective data encryption, key exchange, and digital signature capabilities despite using comparatively smaller keys. This leads to better performance and lower energy usage which makes ECC relevant for mobile and cloud computing environments.
- **Secure Hash Algorithm 2 (SHA-2):** SHA-2 refers to the group of cryptographic hash functions used for creating fixed-size hashes out of data. Hashes are useful in checking the integrity of information by detecting any modifications during storage or transmission. SHA-2 underpins the processes of digital signatures and SSL/TLS certificates.

The choice of algorithm affects the speed, strength, and applicability of your cryptographic systems.

Protocols

Protocols define how cryptographic methods are applied to real-world scenarios, such as secure communication or authentication. In other words, protocols are instructions that describe how a cryptographic algorithm works. Examples include:

- **Transport Layer Security**: TLS is the foundation of secure communication over the internet. It protects data in transit — such as between browsers and servers — by encrypting it and verifying the identities of both parties. TLS is the technology behind the HTTPS protocol, and it is also extensively utilized in email and instant messaging applications.
- **Internet Protocol Security (IPSec):** The IPSec protocol offers protection for data at the network level, thus providing significant advantages when implementing secure tunnels in virtual private networks (VPNs). Every IP packet within the session is authenticated and encrypted by the IPSec protocol to guarantee safe transfer.
- **Secure/Multipurpose Internet Mail Extensions (S/MIME):** S/MIME provides email messages with end-to-end encryption and digital signatures to ensure that only the designated receiver will be able to open the message and confirm that no unauthorized modifications have been made to the message during transmission.

They play a vital role in protecting all kinds of activities, ranging from e-banking and telecommuting to enterprise systems and machine communications.

Cryptographic Infrastructure

Cryptographic systems combine protocols, algorithms, and methods into an architecture for handling cryptographic processes on a larger scale. Some examples of this infrastructure include:

- **Public Key Infrastructure (PKI):** PKI is the framework used to generate, manage, and revoke digital certificates. It allows users, devices, and services to authenticate themselves through the use of a public key tied to their identity. PKI is essential to the trust model in many applications, such as websites, emails, and software signing.

- **Hardware Security Modules (HSMs):** HSMs are specialized hardware appliances designed to protect keys through secure storage and management of cryptographic functions. They offer a physical root of trust for sensitive cryptographic processes and are mandatory in industries requiring a high degree of assurance, such as banking and government.
- **Keys Management Systems:** Keys management systems ensure that keys are managed throughout their lifecycle, from generation to destruction. They offer centralized management, which enables organizations to enforce policies, minimize errors, and comply with regulations within cloud, on-premise, and hybrid infrastructures.

All of this infrastructure elements combined ensure that cryptographically-enabled controls not only remain secure, but scalable, enforceable, and auditable as well.

2.3.3. CRYPTOGRAPHY USE CASES

Cryptography helps provide secure experiences in almost any sector or online activity you can imagine. Whether you're sending an encrypted email or ensuring that your device can authenticate itself to access a network, cryptography is doing its work.

Some ways that companies employ cryptography include:

1. **Digital Payments**

   Every time a consumer makes a purchase using a credit card or their mobile device through an online payment system or a point-of-sale terminal, cryptography is at play. Cryptography provides encryption of data transmitted through the internet and validates transactions through digital signatures and tokenization processes.

2. **Communication Security**

   The use of cryptography in applications such as instant messaging services, web conferencing applications, and email applications ensures that messages sent between the two parties are encrypted. The process of encryption ensures that only the intended recipient has access to the message.

3. **Electronic Signature Processes**

   The use of cryptography in the form of digital signatures allows one to sign documents digitally, ensuring that the integrity of the document is maintained and any attempts to alter the document can be detected.

4. **Code Signing**

   Before deploying software updates or applications, developers use digital signatures to certify that the code hasn't been altered. Devices and systems can then verify these signatures before installation. This protects users from malware disguised as legitimate software and helps maintain trust in the software supply chain.

5. **Regulatory Compliance**

   Encryption technology can help organizations achieve compliance with regulations that require protection of sensitive data and include HIPAA, GDPR, and PCI-DSS. Companies implement encryption and authentication to protect their confidential information and comply with legal regulations.

In conclusion, it is necessary to say that cryptography has a number of important applications which make it significant for protecting sensitive data and information and maintaining cybersecurity and safe communication.

2.3.4. KEY MANAGEMENT AND CRYPTOGRAPHIC CHALLENGES

The strength of encryption depends on the strength of the keys used for encryption. This makes the management of cryptographic keys vital to any cryptographic security system. This means that no matter how strong the encryption is, it will fail if its cryptographic keys are not managed properly. Some of the threats involved include:

- **Ad Hoc Cryptography Keys:** Hybrid clouds and multi-clouds make it easy for companies to produce keys through ad hoc means in different teams and departments. This leads to key proliferation, duplications, poor management, and lack of visibility.
- **Hidden Cryptography Tools:** Cryptography tools are often deployed by developers without the knowledge of the IT department or the relevant security body. The deployment process is difficult to trace and audit. Such an implementation may result in exposure due to lack of adherence to security best practices.
- **Expiry of Certificates:** Certificates that are used for authentication and securing connections should be renewed periodically. However, when they expire unnoticed, such as what happened in the case of the Equifax breach in 2017, the effect could be fatal since they may break connections or lead to coverage vulnerabilities.
- **Lack of Visibility:** In most cases, enterprises cannot answer some critical questions regarding their keys and certificates. These include what happens to the keys and certificates, whether they are being rotated as recommended, and who accesses them.

Such problems may result in expensive downtime, audit failures, and even security vulnerabilities.

However, there is a solution – the Cryptographic Security Platform from Entrust. It solves the mentioned problems due to its capability to provide visibility, enforce policies, and automate the key lifecycle. The consolidation of all cryptographic tasks into one platform makes key management more efficient and secure (Kayem et al., 2010).

2.3.5. DIGITAL SIGNATURES FOR NON-REPUDIATION

In order to achieve non-repudiation, a security feature that guarantees that a party cannot contest the legitimacy or source of a digital communication or document they have signed, digital signatures are essential.

Examples

- Digital signatures can be created using the popular asymmetric encryption method known as RSA (Rivest-Shamir-Adleman).

Use: Key exchange, secure communication, and digital signatures.

- Elliptic curve cryptography is used in the DSA variant known as ECDSA (Elliptic Curve Digital Signature Algorithm).

Use: Secure communication and digital signatures.

Types of Cryptography:

There are two types of cryptography

1. **Symmetric Cryptography:**

   Both encryption and decryption employ the same secret key.

   When parties can safely exchange a key, it is effective for handling massive amounts of data.

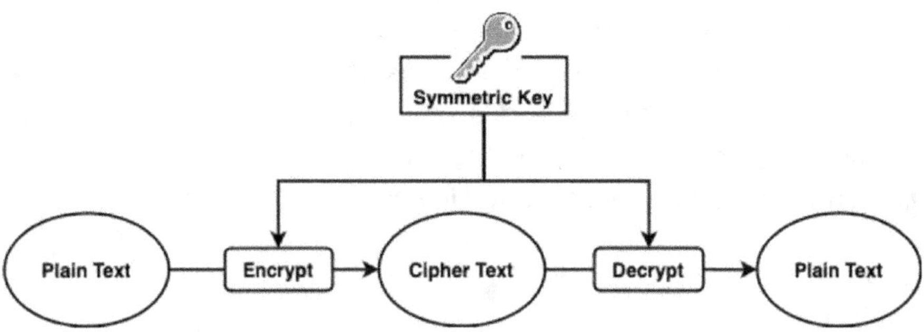

Figure 2.2: Symmetric Key Encryption Process

The symmetric encryption method, which uses the same secret key to both encrypt plaintext into ciphertext and decrypt it back into readable form, is shown in figure 2.2.

2. **Asymmetric Cryptography:**

   It makes use of a set of public and private keys. The private key is used for decryption, while the public key is used for encryption.

   digital signatures, secure communication over unsecure channels, and key exchange.

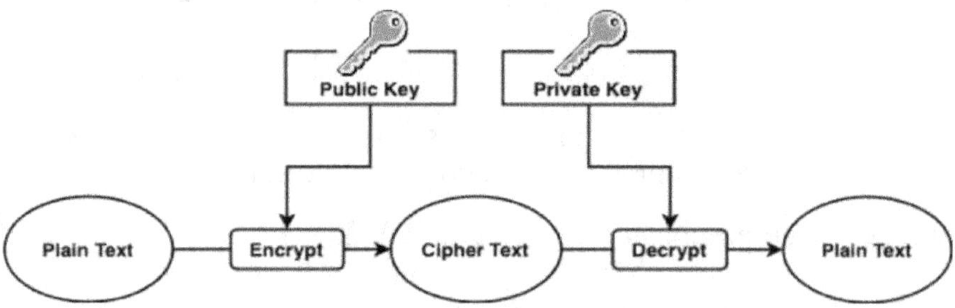

Figure 2.3: Asymmetric (Public-Key) Encryption

This figure 2.3 method, a **public key** encrypts the plain text into cipher text, while a separate **private key** decrypt it back — ensuring only the intended recipient can read the message.

In summary, digital signatures and cryptography technologies have an important place in securing communications, authentication, and non-repudiation within digital environments. The use of symmetric and asymmetric cryptography ensures that sensitive data remains confidential and protected from any potential breach, whereas digital signatures guarantee that the content of an electronic message is both authentic and has not been altered in any way.

2.4. RISK ASSESSMENT IN HEALTHCARE DATA PRIVACY

The process of assessing the possible dangers connected to an organization's data assets is known as data risk assessment. This involves identifying the type of information collected, its storage location, who has access to it, and how it can be used.

One proactive measure adopted by health care organizations to identify risks and vulnerabilities concerning patients' privacy is the health care privacy risk assessment. This evaluation is evaluating how well the company's current technologies, policies, processes, and systems protect sensitive data.

By carrying out an evaluation, healthcare providers can learn about potential vulnerabilities that could jeopardize patient privacy and put in place the appropriate safeguards and controls to successfully reduce these risks.

2.4.1. DATA RISK ASSESSMENT EXPLAINED

The process of data risk assessment entails a complete review of an organization's data environment to determine any risks, weaknesses, or threats arising from the handling, processing, storage, and dissemination of confidential data, especially those in cloud computing. This helps in the identification of security measures that would be critical for reducing the chances of data loss and data breach and will also assist in ensuring regulatory compliance.

Some of the key steps that are involved in performing a data risk assessment are carrying out data inventory and classification, which involve identifying the types of data available within the organization and the type of data that needs further protection. Another important step is carrying out a security assessment on the existing security controls.

Next, examining the possibility of various threats, such as breaches, leakage, or any unintentional exposure of information, helps in addressing remediation of the issues. Other considerations include regulatory compliance and industry standards that should be considered in order to effectively manage risk.

After identification and prioritization of risks, the next step would be implementation of the necessary risk control mechanisms, such as encryption and access controls. Monitoring of the environment will allow for the identification of any newly introduced risks.

Ultimately, having an incident response plan in place along with the review of the data risk assessment process will help businesses stay on top of changing threats and remain proactive in their approaches to protecting their data. With the help of conducting data risk assessments and applying customized security measures, organizations will be able to secure their data from breaches.

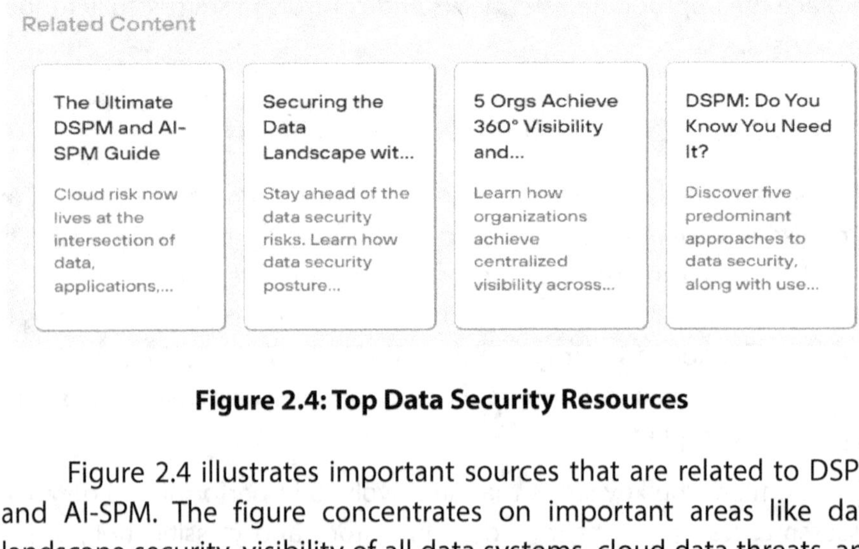

Figure 2.4: Top Data Security Resources

Figure 2.4 illustrates important sources that are related to DSPM and AI-SPM. The figure concentrates on important areas like data landscape security, visibility of all data systems, cloud data threats, and many other important aspects concerning data security. Such sources are useful for organizations seeking ways to enhance data security and protect themselves from any risks in data management.

Overall, it can be stated that data risk assessment is a very important practice aimed at revealing potential dangers related to the use of certain data within the organization. Data classification, assessment of security measures, threat identification, and monitoring are just some activities that contribute to a more robust data protection strategy and prevent any data leaks (Hoffmann et al., 2017).

2.4.2. WHEN ASSESSING RISK IS NECESSARY

The risk of data breaches, cyberattacks, and regulatory compliance issues is greater than ever due to the growing volume of data collected and stored. Organisations can gain a thorough understanding of their data assets, vulnerabilities, and the possible consequences of a security incident or data breach by performing a data risk analysis. This information helps them prioritize investments in data security measures and informs their risk management approach.

There is never a one-size-fits-all approach to managing data protection risks; instead, each company must make its own decisions. Assessing and managing various kinds of data risks is required by some organizations' procedures. Certain tasks, like cybersecurity, will be shared by all organisations. Others, including compliance, will depend on the industry vertical and the kinds of data that are processed and kept.

An example of several business procedures that could result in evaluating data risks is as follows:

- **Compliance:** Organisations must identify and manage data risks in accordance with several requirements. Managing and lowering data risks can assist guarantee adherence to laws like PCI DSS, GDPR, and HIPAA.
- **Cybersecurity:** Security evaluations aid in the detection and control of cybersecurity threats, including ransomware attacks, illegal access, and data breaches. Organisations can tailor their controls to minimize risk by identifying sensitive data types, such as financial or personally identifiable information (PII).
- **Data governance:** Companies can ensure data accuracy, completeness, and integrity by employing data risk management, which is important for decision-making.

- **Cloud migration:** With companies increasingly transferring data to the cloud, data risk management can ensure that data is secure and compliant during and after the transition.
- **Third-party risk management:** It is common practice for companies to outsource data to third parties, which poses a significant threat to the occurrence of data breaches. Data risk management can help mitigate such risks and secure data.
- **Mergers and acquisitions:** During such processes, data transfer takes place from one company to another. This introduces additional data risks. Data risk management can help ensure security and compliance throughout the process.

Risk assessment is an important process that organizations undertake in order to assess possible threats and secure their data. Risk assessments help organizations implement proper security measures and prevent any possible breach of data. Through the identification of such risks as cybersecurity, cloud computing, third-party providers, and data governance, organizations are able to manage these risks effectively and promote the privacy and security of their sensitive data.

2.4.3. BENEFITS OF ASSESSING DATA RISK

In order to make economical cybersecurity decisions, risk assessments of data are important. Organisations need to make deliberate decisions that will enable them to implement security successfully owing to financial constraints. Organisations face various challenges, among them being the prevention of data abuse, non-compliance with standards, and data leakage for data stored both in on-premises and cloud-based platforms.

With data risk assessments, organisations will be able to get a complete view of the status of their data and its risk posture. There is no way that data can be secured without first understanding what the organization has and its current level of risk posture. These assessments provide information that enables the organization to coordinate its security policies and deal with high-risk items, thereby reducing the likelihood of experiencing a data breach or data exfiltration event while ensuring that they follow industry standards.

Data Security Improvement: In assessing data risk, organisations will be able to implement measures meant to mitigate the identified data security risks.

- **Regulatory Compliance:** Organizations need to carry out risk assessments because there are several sectors that necessitate organizations to do so. With the help of data risk assessment, organizations can identify any compliance issues and be sure about whether they are compliant with regulatory requirements.
- **Saving Costs:** Organizational risk assessments can help the organization save costs associated with a data breach, such as loss of revenue, legal fees, and damaged reputation.
- **Better Decision Making:** With the help of data risk assessment, organizations can have a complete understanding of their data security status. In addition, the organization can make informed decisions about implementing and prioritizing data security measures.
- **Building Customer Trust:** Organizations can build the trust of their customers by carrying out regular risk assessments, thereby demonstrating commitment towards data security. The reputation of an organization will thus be enhanced.
- **Proactive Steps:** Risk assessments for data security can help organizations become more proactive towards data security.

Assessing Risk in Cloud Data

Risk assessment for cloud data is now considered one of the most essential elements of data security management. As more sensitive data continues to be stored in the cloud by organizations, the importance of recognizing the dangers associated with these data sets increases exponentially. In cloud data, risk assessment involves:

- Determining the types of data that are stored in order to identify security and privacy requirements

- Identifying potential vulnerabilities and deviations from organizational requirements or industry standards
- Leveraging the risk posture to determine the likelihood and potential impacts of the attack

Security threats may be detected and dealt with far in advance through analysis of the security protocols put in place to protect the data, along with identification of any vulnerabilities within your organization. This risk assessment process is largely automated through the use of Data Security Posture Management (DSPM) solutions, providing organizations with continuous insight into cloud data threats and ensuring they maintain accurate knowledge of their security posture.

Organisations may better protect their cloud data and lower the risk of data breaches, data exfiltration, non-compliance, and cyberattacks by conducting regular risk assessments and implementing bespoke controls.

Data risk evaluation is an essential activity that assists companies in improving their data protection measures, complying with regulations, and making wise decisions regarding their cybersecurity. Through risk evaluations, organizations are able to detect weak spots in their operations and put necessary measures to protect themselves from data breaches and cyber threats. Effective risk evaluation leads to increased customer confidence, improved efficiencies, and proactive management of sensitive data (Catt, 2018).

2.4.4. THE IMPORTANCE OF A PRIVACY IMPACT ASSESSMENT IN HEALTHCARE

A key component of any healthcare system is privacy. Patients entrust their most personal information to medical providers, expecting it to be kept private and discreet. However, preserving patient trust has grown more difficult due to the growing digitization of medical records and the rise in cyber risks.

Health care organizations can benefit from privacy impact evaluations in the following ways:

- **Determine vulnerability:** Through extensive evaluations of existing processes, health care facilities will be able to identify which processes pose threats to the privacy of patients. These may include examining the use of EHRs, storage of information, accessibility by employees, and contracts with vendors.
- **Prioritize:** After identifying vulnerable processes, health care facilities will be able to determine the level of priority according to the severity of the threats against the privacy of the patients.
- **Mitigation Strategies:** After the understanding of the possible threats and the prioritization process, the organization should be able to put measures in place to prevent any form of risk from occurring. It can involve putting encryption mechanisms in place, strengthening the training of employees, and setting access protocols.

Regulatory Compliance: Privacy Impact Assessments are a must in ensuring that patient data is protected and compliance with the regulatory requirements set by bodies like HIPAA is met (Singh & Kumar, 2024).

2.4.5. PRIVACY IMPACT ASSESSMENT TEMPLATE IN HEALTHCARE

The PIA Template is used as a tool to assist healthcare organizations in conducting their privacy impact assessment. Although PIA Templates can differ based on individual organizational requirements, the following areas are typically addressed:

- **Information gathering:** Evaluate how the organization gathers, stores and transmits patient information. Information gathering would include an evaluation of consent, data retention, and security aspects of information collection.
- **Information access:** Identify who has access to patient information and when access takes place. Review user accounts, authentication methods and auditing processes to

determine whether the correct personnel have the capability to view the information.

- **Information security:** Review the organization's practices regarding the protection of patient information from access, exposure or disclosure. Security measures could include the use of encryption, anti-virus, firewalls, and disaster recovery strategies.
- **External relationships:** Consider any organizations that have access to the patient information or provide some kind of service in relation to the processing or storage of information.
- **Risk Analysis:** Perform a risk analysis where all possible risks that may affect patient privacy are analyzed. Rank them according to priority depending on the severity and probability of the risk occurring.
- **Plan Mitigation Actions:** Plan actions to mitigate risks and ensure the risks are addressed in the most efficient way possible.

In summary, it is clear that the PIA template acts as an essential tool for healthcare organizations in ensuring that privacy risks related to patients' information are systematically identified, analyzed, and managed. Issues such as data collection, access controls, data security, risk assessment, and risk management strategies need to be adequately covered using the PIA template to increase data security and ensure compliance with existing data privacy laws and guidelines.

2.5. CHAPTER SUMMARY

This chapter reviewed some of the key approaches towards ensuring privacy through data protection and management in the contemporary world of technology. It started with explaining the process of anonymization and de-identification, which explained how entities stripped themselves of personally identifiable information (PII). Methods of anonymization included data masking, pseudonymization, data aggregation, generalization, data generation, and data swapping; the methods were explained, and their use cases in the healthcare, finance, telecommunication, and government industries were identified.

Finally, the benefits and drawbacks of each approach were analyzed, while recognizing that the de-identification technique-maintained data integrity while anonymization destroyed it. The balance between privacy and utility was highlighted in the context of the healthcare industry.

Moreover, the topic of differential privacy was discussed in the chapter as an advanced mathematical technique that helps ensure data security without restricting the analysis process. The chapter shed light on how differential privacy operates by injecting noise into the data and what advantages it provides in terms of privacy guarantees, defense against privacy attacks, and customizable levels of privacy. Challenges faced by the topic, as well as applications by entities like Google, Apple, and the U.S. Census Bureau, were also highlighted in the chapter.

Besides, cryptography was another important area covered in the chapter. Specifically, the chapter provided detailed coverage of data protection techniques such as encryption, hashing, digital signatures, and authentication. Some of the key cryptographic concepts discussed in the chapter include symmetric/asymmetric encryption, algorithms, security protocols, and key management systems.

Finally, there was an analysis of risk assessment in the context of data privacy in the healthcare sector. The chapter explained how risk assessment and privacy impact assessment (PMA) are integral parts of any organization since they help identify potential risks and weaknesses and also help stay compliant. The authors also stressed that proper risk assessments, appropriate controls, and privacy management practices are important for protecting health data from cybersecurity threats. In conclusion, this chapter showed that privacy protection techniques and cryptographic methods as well as proper risk assessment are key for any information protection.

Multiple Choice Questions (MCQs)

1. **What is the primary goal of data anonymization?**
   - A. Increase data storage capacity
   - B. Protect individual identity in datasets
   - C. Improve data accuracy
   - D. Speed up data processing
2. **Which technique removes personally identifiable information (PII) from datasets?**
   - A. Encryption
   - B. De-identification
   - C. Compression
   - D. Indexing
3. **In data anonymization, what does "k-anonymity" ensure?**
   - A. Data is encrypted with k keys
   - B. Each record is identical
   - C. Each individual is indistinguishable from at least k-1 others
   - D. Data cannot be accessed
4. **What is a key feature of differential privacy?**
   - A. It completely removes all data
   - B. It adds controlled noise to data
   - C. It encrypts data permanently
   - D. It stores data offline

5. **Differential privacy helps in:**

   A. Eliminating databases

   B. Sharing data without revealing individual information

   C. Increasing data duplication

   D. Preventing all cyberattacks

6. **Which cryptographic method uses the same key for encryption and decryption?**

   A. Asymmetric cryptography

   B. Hashing

   C. Symmetric cryptography

   D. Digital signatures

7. **What is the purpose of hashing in data protection?**

   A. To compress data

   B. To convert data into a fixed-length value

   C. To encrypt data with keys

   D. To store data securely

8. **Which of the following is an example of asymmetric cryptography?**

   A. AES

   B. DES

   C. RSA

   D. MD5

9. **In healthcare data privacy, risk assessment primarily focuses on:**

   A. Increasing patient data size

   B. Identifying potential privacy breaches

   C. Reducing hospital costs

   D. Improving treatment methods

10. **What is a major risk in healthcare data sharing?**

    A. Data redundancy

    B. Re-identification of anonymized data

    C. Data compression loss

    D. Network slowdown

Answers

1	2	3	4	5	6	7	8	9	10
B	B	C	B	B	C	B	C	B	B

Chapter 3

FEDERATED LEARNING IN HEALTHCARE

3.1. INTRODUCTION TO FEDERATED LEARNING

The Federated Learning is a kind of machine learning technique that involves collaborative training of a single global model by several clients or servers without transferring the underlying data set. Under this technique, each node trains the underlying model locally on their own data sets and updates only parameters or models to a central server, which helps enhance the global model through aggregated updates.

On the other hand, artificial intelligence models usually need substantial data sets for efficient training. However, data in such cases is always held in one place and therefore prone to data breach, leakage, and unauthorized access during storage or transmission. Federated Learning helps overcome the problem as it holds data locally but collaborates for training purposes. Therefore, several servers, institutions, or devices can participate in enhancing the model by collaborating.

3.1.1. NEED FOR FEDERATED LEARNING IN HEALTHCARE

Healthcare federated learning facilitates the training of AI algorithms without transferring the private health data of patients to different hospitals and institutes. This method involves bringing the AI algorithm to the location where the relevant data is located rather than moving data to a central location. Key benefits include improved privacy protection, simplified regulatory compliance (HIPAA, GDPR), improved model performance from diverse datasets, reduced bias, and cost efficiency by avoiding data centralization.

The importance of Federated Learning is particularly evident in pharmaceutical research and clinical trial collaboration, where data sensitivity and intellectual property protection are major concerns. Pharmaceutical companies are now aware that working together with hospitals and rivals may be the key to stopping this trend, from finding drug leads to enhancing clinical trial design to tracking patient outcomes.

However, the sector faces significant obstacles due to privacy and intellectual property protection concerns. Due to the sensitivity and importance of these clinical datasets, data from pharma-sponsored clinical trials are often only accessible to the sponsor until the trial is over.

In a similar vein, pharmaceutical companies' "chemical libraries," which are priceless collections of compounds utilized for internal drug development, are not put up for sharing. Furthermore, many pharmaceutical companies rely on exclusive agreements with tech companies to safeguard their discoveries, and they have not yet implemented machine learning technology at scale due to the time-consuming nature of developing internal expertise. Therefore, the potential of data and insight exchange between pharmaceutical businesses has not yet been achieved, despite the growing demand for AI (Raza, 2023).

3.1.2. WORKING PROCESS OF FEDERATED LEARNING

The federated learning technique is based on the decentralized training approach, where several clients train a common model through collaboration without any exchange of raw data. There are various steps involved in this process, such as initializing the model, local training of the model, aggregating the models globally, and model iterations.

Federated learning involves 4 main stages:

- Initialization
- Local training

- Global aggregation
- Iteration

1. **Initialization**

   Initializing a global machine learning model on a central server is the first step in federated learning. The federated learning process starts with this model.

   The global model is distributed via the central server to connected client nodes, which may be other servers or edge devices like Internet of Things (IoT) devices and smartphones. Additionally, it transmits pertinent data, such as the number of epochs or full runs of the training data and configuration variables like hyperparameters.

2. **Local training**

   Each client node starts training after obtaining the global model and all required information. Similar to any neural network, client nodes use only their local or on-device data to train the model.

   Client nodes provide the updated model parameters or gradients to the central server after completing the required number of epochs; neither raw data nor completely trained local models are returned.

3. **Global aggregation**

   All of the client node updates are combined by the central server. Federated averaging, which determines the weighted average of all updates, is a popular technique among the various types of aggregation. The global model then incorporates these combined changes.

4. **Repeating**

   The federated learning procedure is repeated until the model obtains full convergence or is fully trained after the central server sends the updated global model to linked client nodes once more.

On the whole, Federated Learning allows several clients or parties to learn from the same machine learning algorithm together while maintaining confidentiality of data. Through a decentralized learning process that involves training on individual parties and model aggregation, Federated Learning minimizes threats posed by the storage of data in a single location while ensuring that artificial intelligence algorithms developed in the healthcare environment comply with data protection laws.

3.2. ARCHITECTURE AND WORKFLOW

Federated Learning (FL) implements its architectural design and operational procedures to support cooperative machine learning activities without requiring partner organizations to share their complete unprocessed data. Federated learning takes place through a decentralized system whereby healthcare institutions can keep their data safe while at the same time share updates of the models without consolidating all of the data into a single database. The design of such a system holds vital importance for the healthcare sector since the hospitals, diagnosis centers, and research institutions have to observe strict security protocols to safeguard their patients' data, which is protected by privacy policies.

A standard federated learning framework includes a central server which connects to various client nodes that represent hospitals and medical research facilities and wearable technology and healthcare providers. The central server establishes a global machine learning model which it sends to all client participants. Each client performs local model training with its healthcare data before transmitting only the model updates back to the central server. The server uses Federated Averaging (FedAvg) and other algorithms to aggregate these updates into an enhanced global model. The process of developing the model through this method will keep running until the model reaches its required accuracy and convergence point.

The federated learning workflow provides several advantages for healthcare AI systems, which include better privacy protection and decreased data transmission needs and improved institutional collaboration and regulatory compliance with HIPAA and GDPR. The system design creates difficulties for developers because it hampers communication and synchronization and prevents effective model aggregation and security measures. The architecture and workflow of Federated Learning must be understood by researchers who want to create secure and scalable and efficient healthcare AI systems.

The architecture and communication workflow of Federated Learning in healthcare systems are illustrated in Figure 3.1.

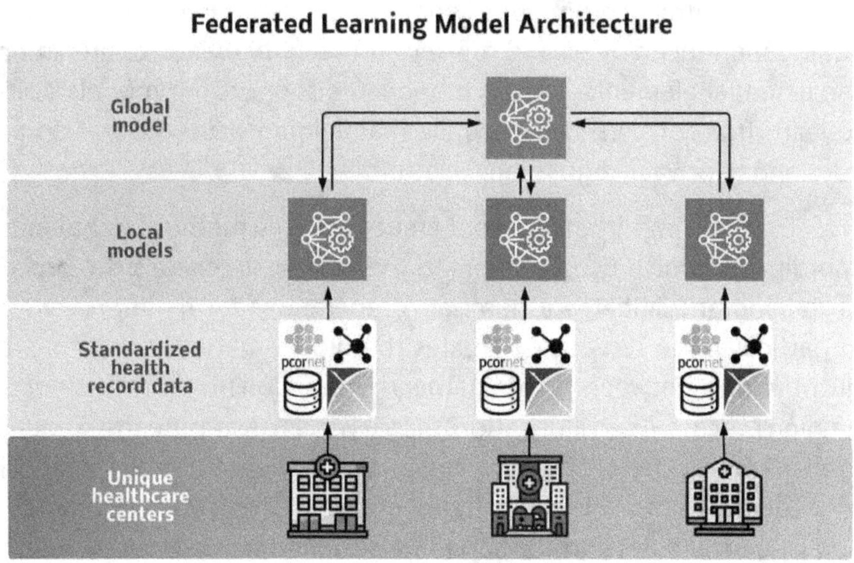

Figure 3.1: Federated Learning Architecture for Healthcare Collaboration

The architecture and process flow of federated learning within healthcare systems are illustrated in Figure 3.1. Local models are trained on client machines such as hospitals and medical devices using their respective data. The only information that is shared from the clients to the central server is the model updates.

In summary, the framework and process of Federated Learning offer a highly secure and decentralized approach to the development of collaborative machine learning models for healthcare organizations. The ability to perform local data training and exchange only model weights helps in ensuring that patients' data is protected while at the same time increasing the efficiency of the models created (Weske et al., 1996).

3.2.1. COMPONENTS OF FEDERATED LEARNING ARCHITECTURE

Machine learning models can be trained across dispersed devices or servers without exchanging raw data thanks to a federated learning system. A central coordinator, client devices, communication protocols, aggregation techniques, and privacy and security measures are among the essential elements. These components support the models' ability to learn from dispersed data while maintaining data localization and adhering to privacy regulations.

Firstly, an important element of such learning methods is the central coordinator (which usually refers to the server). It controls the process of training and initiates a number of operations for its improvement. In particular, the server first creates the global model, and then, after distributing it between clients, gathers information from them about the training process. As an illustration, the server can distribute the language model among the client's devices in the case of a mobile keyboard application. Then each client trains the model on his own device by applying local data, and the server gets the model updates (gradients) from the clients.

The second piece is the client infrastructure, consisting of the devices or servers used for local training. The clients should possess enough computing power for performing training iterations as well as memory to hold the data temporarily. For example, within a federated learning framework for healthcare applications, the hospitals can be treated as clients, who would train the model locally using their patients' data while keeping sensitive information private. The client software usually contains an iterative training loop for performing the optimization process (for example, stochastic gradient descent) and secure data exchange. In order to optimize the consumption of computing resources, methods such as quantization (limiting the precision of updates) or sparse updates (transmitting only important parameters) may be utilized.

The third element is the communication and security stack, which guarantees dependable data transmission. Efficient and reliable communication protocols should be used, even when working with thousands of IoT devices. For instance, protocols such as HTTP/2 or gRPC can be employed for efficient two-way communication. Encryption methods (such as TLS for transit) and aggregation protocols that guarantee data security by using algorithms like homomorphic encryption or multiparty computation should be employed to protect against attacks, making it impossible for the attacker to infer anything about the data being used to train the model from the updates.

Table 3.1: Major Components of Federated Learning Architecture in Healthcare

Component	Function	Healthcare Example
Central Server	Coordinates global model training and aggregation	Cloud-based hospital coordination server
Client Nodes	Perform local model training using private data	Hospitals, research labs, IoMT devices
Communication Layer	Transfers encrypted model updates	HTTPS, gRPC, TLS
Aggregation Algorithm	Combines local model updates	Federated Averaging (FedAvg)
Privacy Mechanisms	Protect sensitive healthcare data	Differential Privacy, Secure Aggregation
Local Dataset	Stores institution-specific healthcare data	EHRs, MRI scans, lab reports

The main Federated Learning architecture components and their corresponding roles in healthcare systems are shown in Table 3.1. Together, the system's various components provide a safe training environment that safeguards user privacy while developing decentralized AI models.

In general, the elements that form part of the Federated Learning architecture are able to collaborate with each other to facilitate learning from multiple healthcare systems in a safe, efficient, and private manner. The architecture is designed in such a way that sensitive information from one institution does not leave the institution but is still able to contribute to the development of the global model.

3.2.2. CLIENT–SERVER COMMUNICATION AND MODEL AGGREGATION

Communication in federated learning is organized in such a way that collaboration in model training takes place without any transfer of raw data. The server organizes and facilitates this process through communication that includes sending out the global model to clients for training. In return, the trained models are sent back to the server, where their values are analyzed to enhance the global model. Communication is done using regular channels such as HTTP/HTTPS and gRPC, with data being secured using encryption methods. For instance, the server can make use of TLS to encrypt the transferred data, while the clients use tokens or certificates as means of verification.

The computations are mostly done locally by the clients, which decreases the computational burden on the server. Once the client gets the global model, it trains based on the local data it has access to and passes the updated weights back to the server. To save on bandwidth, methods such as gradient compression and gradient scarification are usually used. For example, a phone may learn a keyboard predictive model and only pass the top 10% of the gradients to the server. In addition, the server needs to deal with the irregularity in the availability of the clients, with some clients being absent or delayed.

Averages of the client updates are calculated through various mechanisms, including Federated Averaging (FedAvg), which calculates an average of the model weights from the clients in proportion to their data set sizes. Updates can also be secured via protocols that implement homomorphic encryption or secure multiparty computation. The Google Gboard app uses a masking method where updates are summed up before the actual encryption process takes place. Other software frameworks like FLSim from PyTorch and OpenFL offer capabilities for controlling the communication workflow, allowing retries from failed clients, and improving the networking process.

3.2.3. DATA FLOW AND TRAINING WORKFLOW

The data flow and training workflow of Federated Learning (FL) operate to support machine learning collaboration which does not require raw data to be sent to a central server. Federated learning allows training to occur in a decentralized manner because it keeps all data on the local devices of hospitals and healthcare institutions instead of using a central storage system. The system design provides a solution to privacy challenges and security issues together with compliance requirements which arise from centralized AI training processes.

A central server starts the federated learning process by sending out a global machine learning model which clients will use for training. The base model creation process begins with a generic dataset which leads to model distribution among client devices and local server systems. The clients include hospitals and mobile healthcare devices and Internet of Medical Things (IoMT) devices and research institutions which possess essential healthcare information. The client trains the model by using its internal dataset while it protects patient confidentiality through data retention.

The model is trained on local datasets through iterative updates during local training. The training results from each client node create updates which people commonly call gradients or model parameters. The system transmits only the updated model parameters instead of sending back all the data to the central server. Privacy is preserved in the framework because no patient data leaves the client device. The central server aggregates the models received from clients to produce a more powerful global model using the technique known as model aggregation. Model aggregation represents the combined learning that takes place from all the participants in the model development. Clients get back the improved global model that they will use in their next round of local training. The model development process goes on through rounds of local training and parameter sharing, then aggregation and distribution of the model until it achieves sufficient accuracy and convergence across multiple datasets.

The entire AI training process is improved by Federated Learning as it allows for decentralization of learning while ensuring privacy and eliminating any security risks associated with it as well as learning from diverse sources. FL provides an effective solution for healthcare organizations due to its ability to protect patient privacy as well as meet legal requirements.

3.2.4. SECURITY MECHANISMS IN FL ARCHITECTURE

In order to safeguard data, stop exploitation, and reduce dangers, security measures are implemented. Overall, this promotes public confidence and trust in the suggested solution. The risks and dangers related to each of the proposed architecture's components (Parameter Server, Clinical client, or Communication infrastructure) are briefly described in Table, along with the mitigation strategy that was chosen. As can be seen, the design decisions made for the suggested system effectively minimize the primary threats that have been identified. For every element of the suggested architecture, a set of security recommendations may be created after the threat identification stage.

- **Parameter Server**

  Authorization procedures, access control for services like the parameter server and MQTT broker, and training intern staff on security procedures are the main requirements in the context of server-side security and operational standards. It is important to note that CERN's network infrastructure already satisfies these established standards, underscoring CERN's suitability as a public PS for FL process.

- **Communication infrastructure**

  Communication integrity and confidentiality, as well as authentication, are the primary criteria for the communication infrastructure. Authentication is provided at the PS through the usage of SSH tunnels, Kerberos authentication, and MQTT authentication primitives. In a similar vein, message integrity and confidentiality are made possible by combining TLS with MQTT.

- **Clinical clients**

  Given that they host sensitive data and each clinical client is built on a different IT infrastructure, potentially implementing various security procedures, the clinical clients are likely the most susceptible part of the suggested design. Many of the related risks can be reduced by the suggested client node design, but other steps should be taken to improve security at the clinical infrastructure. For instance, an access control system that restricts direct access to the machine running the containers must be designed.

The principle of least privileges (PoLP), which states that users should be granted the minimal access levels or permissions necessary to carry out their job tasks, should be applied throughout the design of such an access control system. Additionally, it's critical to regularly do vulnerability assessments and penetration tests on the client's end. In order to apply security fixes on time, it is essential to set up an effective patch management system. Comprehensive logging and monitoring of computer system activity is the second task that must be completed.

3.3. APPLICATIONS IN CLINICAL DATA ANALYSIS

Federated Learning has revolutionized the analysis of clinical data due to its ability to help healthcare providers build Artificial Intelligence models by collaborating while not needing to reveal sensitive patient information. Centralized databases of different healthcare organizations form the basis of conventional healthcare AI models that need data from different hospitals and medical organizations. The use of centralized data sharing poses challenges due to privacy laws, ethical considerations, and the confidentiality of medical records. However, this challenge can be addressed through the use of Federated Learning which helps healthcare organizations build machine learning models locally and only provide updates on their progress to the central server.

Federated Learning for Clinical Data Analysis has increased its popularity in recent years since healthcare providers are able to collect larger amounts of electronic health records (EHR), medical imaging, wearable devices, genomics databases, and Internet of Medical Things (IoMT). FL enables decentralized learning which helps healthcare organizations create precise AI models by using different patient groups and multiple data sources. This cooperative method enhances diagnostic accuracy plus predictive modeling and personalized treatment plans and medical decision support systems all while safeguarding patient information.

Federated Learning has grown in popularity as a field of study for several healthcare applications, including remote patient monitoring, clinical research, medication discovery, disease detection, and medical picture analysis. FL is used by pharmaceutical companies and healthcare institutions to enhance cooperation, speed up medical research, and adhere to privacy laws like GDPR and HIPAA. Some of the most significant uses of Federated Learning in clinical data analysis and their effects on contemporary healthcare systems are covered in the sections that follow (Weske et al., 1996).

3.3.1. MEDICAL IMAGING AND DISEASE DIAGNOSIS

The Artificial Intelligence (AI) and Machine Learning (ML) research fields produced significant technological advancements which transformed radiology, pathology, and genomics. Medical image analysis has achieved outstanding results because AI uses medical images to identify and classify diseases. AI systems develop detection and diagnostic capabilities through pattern recognition based on radiography and computed tomography (CT) scan images. Deep learning and neural network algorithm improvements have shown that AI technology can help radiologists while enhancing their clinical decision-making process.

The research field faces obstacles because medical imaging systems need deep-learning algorithms to have access to extensive and varied training data in order to achieve precise results. Hospitals and imaging centers maintain restricted medical image collections because they lack extensive image libraries and their medical images do not have complete identification. Creating effective annotated training datasets requires dedicated work from radiologists and healthcare professionals because the process demands extensive time and effort to complete.

Federated Learning (FL) solves these problems by creating a system which enables universal model training across multiple healthcare institutions without disclosing protected patient information. The institutions in this collaborative learning system train their models with their medical imaging data while they send model updates to the central server. The healthcare organizations establish a cooperative relationship which enables them to build AI models with high accuracy while they maintain patient confidentiality and safeguard their data.

Federated Learning enables AI models to acquire knowledge from extensive and varied datasets which multiple healthcare institutions provide from their medical facilities situated in different parts of the world. Patient populations demonstrate different profiles at each hospital because of variations in age distribution, gender ratios, ethnicities, and disease patterns, which makes single institution data models unsuitable for handling uncommon medical cases. Federated Learning solves these issues by enhancing external validity together with diagnostic accuracy and the capability of AI systems to operate across various patient groups. The healthcare industry uses this cooperative framework to propel its progress in precision medicine.

Federal Learning has proven its usefulness through multiple studies which showed its value for medical imaging and disease diagnosis. Intel worked with the University of Pennsylvania biomedical imaging center to test federated learning for brain-image segmentation in 2018 by using the BraTS 2018 dataset which contains MRI brain scans of glioma patients. The institutions received the original model for training purposes but they maintained data privacy by conducting their training process. The results achieved through this method showed close similarity to the outcomes produced by standard centralized machine learning systems.

NVIDIA conducted a major experiment through its partnership with King College London which used the BraTS 2018 dataset for research purposes. The study applied differential privacy techniques within the federated learning framework to protect patient confidentiality during collaborative model training. The results showed that Federated Learning provides performance results which match or exceed those of centralized systems while protecting sensitive medical information through data security measures (Iniewski, 2009).

3.3.2. ELECTRONIC HEALTH RECORD (EHR) ANALYSIS

Electronic Health Records (EHRs) function as digital databases which maintain complete patient records that encompass their medical background, diagnostic findings, lab results, prescribed drugs, medical treatments, personal information, and health assessments. There has been an increase in the adoption of Electronic Health Records (EHR) systems in the health sector, leading to the emergence of healthcare data sets that have acted as vital sources for the design of AI/ML models. These models allow healthcare institutions to engage in predictive analytics and disease risk assessment and mortality predictions. Healthcare institutions face challenges in sharing centralized data because EHR information contains highly sensitive data which privacy regulations strictly control.

Federated Learning (FL) enables multiple hospitals and healthcare organizations to collaboratively train machine learning models using distributed EHR datasets while preserving patient confidentiality. Each organization in this decentralized system builds its AI system through local EHR data training while sending model parameter updates to a main server. The global model is generated by integrating these improvements without having to see any confidential data about patients. The architecture helps the organization carry out HIPAA and GDPR-compliant healthcare analytics without breaching patient confidentiality.

Federated Learning has been extensively studied to create clinical prediction models and to perform healthcare analytics through the analysis of EHR data. The primary use of this technology involves predicting death rates among individuals who have contracted COVID-19. The researchers created federated learning models through the analysis of EHR data which they collected from different hospitals that operate within the Mount Sinai Health System located in New York City. The research study analyzed patient demographics and medical history together with laboratory results and vital signs and showed that federated models achieved better results than locally developed models when they predicted patient mortality within seven days of hospital admission. These results demonstrated that FL technology enables better predictive performance because it allows systems to develop better models through their access to healthcare data which remains protected.

Federated Learning enhances both fairness and generalization capabilities of EHR analysis through its ability to let AI systems acquire knowledge from various patient groups who receive treatment at different healthcare facilities. Single hospital healthcare datasets fail to provide complete population representation because their demographic and disease distribution and medical treatment methods differ from those found in the general population. Distributed EHR systems enable organizations to work together which helps decrease bias while enhancing external validity and achieving better clinical predictions for different patient populations.

There are many advantages offered by federated learning in EHR analysis, but there are also many disadvantages, such as heterogeneous datasets and loss of clinical data and interoperability issues and increased communication complexity and security concerns. Since the different hospitals use distinct EHR standards and data formats, this causes barriers in data integration and consistency of models between the systems. In order to solve interoperability and security challenges, researches and practitioners look into using FHIR as a standard of interoperability, as well as investigating differential privacy and secure aggregation and decentralized federated learning (Data & others, 2016).

3.3.3. DRUG DISCOVERY AND CLINICAL RESEARCH

A decentralized machine learning system called federated learning allows several organisations to collaboratively train ML models without needing access to the data. FL allows data to be kept across multiple devices or servers to maintain its security and confidentiality, in contrast to centralized data storage in a single location. It suggests that data from several pharmaceutical companies can be combined to create models in the field of drug discovery without jeopardizing patient records or other datasets.

Key components of FL include:

- **Local Training:** Each participant trains a model on their local data.
- **Model Aggregation:** A central server aggregates the locally trained models into a global model.
- **Privacy Mechanisms:** Techniques like differential privacy and secure multi-party computation ensure data security during aggregation.

This means that hospitals, research institutions, and pharmaceutical companies will work together to analyze patient data while maintaining patient privacy. The idea is to train the algorithm locally in each dataset before combining them to create a global model. By doing away with the requirement for centralized data storage, this lowers the possibility of data breaches and guarantees adherence to laws like GDPR and HIPAA.

Key concepts include:

- **Decentralized Data Processing:** Only model updates are communicated, while data stays on local servers.
- **Privacy-Preserving Techniques:** Data security is ensured by techniques like safe multi-party computation and differential privacy.
- **Global Model Aggregation:** Creating a cohesive, reliable model by combining local model updates.

- **Cross-Silo and Cross-Device FL:** While cross-device FL concentrates on individual devices, cross-silo FL entails cooperation between organisations.

On the whole, FL is a strong tool to ensure privacy for the processes of discovering drugs and conducting clinical research as it allows hospitals, pharmaceutical firms, and scientific organizations to collaborate while keeping the confidential raw data secret from each other. In particular, FL helps increase the efficiency of research, improve the precision of the models used because of more various datasets, and make sure that the relevant healthcare laws are adhered to (Chorghade, 2006).

3.3.4. REMOTE PATIENT MONITORING AND IOMT

The rapidly expanding discipline of remote patient monitoring (RPM) uses flexible materials for wearable sensors and is intended to help doctors offer treatment in a variety of general hospital medical and surgical wards. This is accomplished by implementing new Internet of Things (IoT) techniques in the healthcare industry, such as wearable technology, contact-based sensors, and telehealth applications. Vital signs and other physiological indicators, such motion recognition, are frequently measured with RPM. These measurements can help with clinical judgements and treatment strategies for problems like psychological disorders or movement disorders.

The networked system of medical devices and applications that gather, process, and send health data is known as the Internet of Medical Things (IoMT). IoMT makes continuous health monitoring and data collecting possible, from wearable fitness trackers and distant monitoring devices to smart hospital equipment. The perpetual stream of data allows healthcare professionals to gain insights into the health status of patients and implement necessary steps for diagnosing and managing diseases.

For instance, let us examine a case in which the patient is diagnosed with diabetes. By equipping the patient with an IoMT-capable glucose meter, it becomes possible to monitor the changes in the levels of sugar and alert the attending physician if there is any abnormality. It would help to avoid serious repercussions by taking preventive measures at the right time.

Federated Learning makes it possible for Remote Patient Monitoring and IoMT platforms to train artificial intelligence models on wearables and healthcare apps and servers since it enables training to occur locally and keeps patients' private health data out of centralized systems.

3.4. BENEFITS AND LIMITATIONS

Federated Learning (FL) has proved to be an essential technique that maintains privacy and creates artificial intelligence (AI) systems that can be applied in the healthcare sector. Through FL hospitals and research organizations together with pharmaceutical firms and medical devices can perform decentralized machine learning to develop AI systems while maintaining the confidentiality of patient information. This method solves major issues which healthcare systems face regarding their security needs and their requirements for maintaining privacy and following regulatory standards.

Federated Learning provides multiple benefits which include better patient privacy protection and better collaborative learning capabilities and increased system scalability and access to various healthcare datasets. The system faces difficulties which include communication overhead and data heterogeneity issues and model bias problems and privacy attacks that impact its effectiveness and dependability. The secure and effective development of healthcare AI applications needs organizations to understand both the advantages and disadvantages of Federated Learning technology.

The major benefits and challenges associated with Federated Learning in healthcare systems are summarized in Table 3.2.

Table 3.2: Benefits and Challenges of Federated Learning in Healthcare

Benefits	**Challenges**
Improved patient privacy	High communication overhead
HIPAA and GDPR compliance	Data heterogeneity
Collaborative AI training	Synchronization issues
Reduced data centralization	Security attacks on model updates
Better model generalization	Complex aggregation mechanisms
Faster clinical research	Infrastructure requirements
Access to diverse datasets	Bias and validation problems
Scalable healthcare AI systems	Network latency

In general, the use of Federated Learning can be considered an ideal technique in developing healthcare AI technologies due to its ability to provide strong privacy protection and collaborative training. However, despite its benefits that include higher data security, regulatory compliance, and improved model performance, there are several disadvantages associated with this technique including poor communication, heterogeneous data sets, and complexity. It is important to overcome these disadvantages in order to implement Federated Learning effectively.

3.4.1. BENEFITS OF FEDERATED LEARNING IN HEALTHCARE

Federated Learning provides several practical and technical benefits in healthcare environments. By enabling decentralized AI training across hospitals, research institutions, and pharmaceutical organizations, FL improves privacy, collaboration, scalability, and healthcare innovation while maintaining regulatory compliance.

1. **Strengthened Data Privacy and Compliance**

   By removing the need to centralize sensitive patient data, a federated learning platform helps you adhere to local,

GDPR, and HIPAA standards. This builds trust both inside and outside the company and significantly lowers the likelihood of breaches.

2. **Availability of Diverse and High-Quality Data**

   AI models need to be trained on a variety of data in order to operate at their best. You can work with a variety of diseases and demographics in Florida without sacrificing data quality. This is crucial, particularly when studying under-represented populations or rare diseases.

3. **Quick Drug Discovery**

   Ten pharmaceutical companies trained models with 10 million chemicals using FL technology through MELLODDY research. The method showed a 30% quicker candidate finding without disclosing private chemical libraries.

4. **Economical and Efficient**

   Expensive data lakes are no longer a necessity. Health care organizations can make use of their current resources, while small hospitals can participate in large research projects.

5. **Effective Collaboration**

   Real-time collaboration becomes possible in federated healthcare learning between doctors, researchers, and data analysts. For example, when training a model for cancer prognosis at a hospital, feedback from oncologists is included immediately.

6. **Competitive Collaboration ("Coopetition")**

   Pharmaceutical firms or hospitals in competition could train models collaboratively yet retain full control over proprietary data – a win for both parties.

7. **Flexible & Scalable Infrastructure**

   Any institution from academic laboratories to country-wide research networks uses federated learning for scalable infrastructure in any type of project, be it imaging, genomics, EHR, or predictive modeling.

8. **Improved Patient Outcome**

   Models trained with FL have already demonstrated improvements in the diagnostics and prognosis of breast cancer, improving patient outcome and care paths.

In summary, FL appears to be an effective and realistic model for driving the development of AI in the health sector by facilitating collaboration between various organizations without compromising patients' confidentiality. Given its ability to facilitate data usage, optimize clinical trials, and guarantee compliance with regulations, FL has tremendous value in the contemporary healthcare sector. Even though there are some difficulties involved, FL is future-proof for the development of medical AI systems (Xhafa, 2024).

3.4.2. CHALLENGES AND SECURITY ISSUES IN FEDERATED LEARNING

Communication Challenges in Federated Learning

- **High Communication Costs**

  The cost of communication, since the transfer of model weights from various data sources incurs quite an amount of communication cost, represents a considerable hurdle in the implementation of Federated Learning. Each step of the learning process requires communication cost in terms of transferring information, which may be too much for many US-based practices to bear.

  It is important, therefore, to adopt an efficient method of communication that reduces communication. Most healthcare organizations have trouble handling electronic health records and other forms of communication.

- **Methodological Flaws and Bias**

  The flaws in methodology and bias in FL research pose significant impediments to the success of FLs. There are various challenges associated with many FL implementations such as lack of sufficient model validation, bias in training data, and reproducibility. These shortcomings could lead to untrustworthy models that would fail to produce the desired clinical results.

In light of the adoption of FL in medicine, it becomes essential to emphasize the importance of robust methodologies in model validation. Through model validation, practices will be able to mitigate data bias.

Security Challenges in Federated Learning

- **Protecting Patient Privacy**

  In the field of healthcare, data privacy is very important; therefore, safeguarding patients' data throughout the process of federated learning becomes highly essential. Sending model parameters from clients' devices to a central server exposes private patient data during transmission.

  Some secure aggregation (SA) mechanisms, including the Joye-Libert and Low Overhead Masking SA schemes, have proven to be beneficial in terms of protecting privacy in federated learning algorithms such as Fed-BioMed. Using these techniques helps reduce privacy leaks without significantly affecting task performance; hence, results obtained have almost no deterioration. The computational overhead for using these protocols is also low, remaining under 1% on CPU and less than 50% on GPU.

Despite these advancements, practical use of secure aggregation is limited due to communication bottlenecks. Therefore, integrating efficient SA protocols into healthcare data management systems must be carefully considered.

Table 3.3: Real-World Case Studies of Federated Learning in Healthcare

Case Study	Application Area	Key Contribution
EXAM AI Model	COVID-19 Prediction	Oxygen requirement prediction using distributed hospital data
Mount Sinai FL	EHR Analysis	Mortality prediction using federated EHR datasets
NVIDIA FLARE	Medical Imaging	Privacy-preserving imaging collaboration
MELLODDY Project	Drug Discovery	Secure pharmaceutical collaboration

Real-life examples of using Federated Learning in the healthcare sector are outlined in Table 3.3 below. Some of the most interesting cases include using Federated Learning to predict the risk of developing COVID-19, analyzing electronic health records (EHRs), conducting medical imaging studies, and searching for new drugs. These examples prove that FL technology is effective in facilitating cooperation between organizations without violating patients' confidentiality.

Generally speaking, Federated Learning entails both numerous possibilities and some difficulties in the context of health care settings. Even though it provides for the opportunity to collaborate safely between parties without compromising patient data, there are such drawbacks to the technology as high communication expenses, data bias, and inconsistent methodology among others. Also, providing for patients' privacy during communication will be an important issue to consider.

3.5. CASE STUDIES IN FEDERATED HEALTHCARE SYSTEMS

Federated Learning (FL) has become an essential technology which enables secure and privacy-protecting Artificial Intelligence (AI) systems for healthcare applications. The healthcare sector together with research institutions and pharmaceutical companies has achieved success in deploying FL frameworks to conduct collaborative machine learning without exposing sensitive patient data. The practical applications of decentralized AI systems show their ability to enhance medical research activities and clinical decision processes and disease prediction methods and medical imaging assessment and drug development research while following healthcare privacy standards which include HIPAA and GDPR regulations.

The case studies present which tools use Federated Learning as their main technology for operating in healthcare environments. The case studies show how hospitals and healthcare networks and pharmaceutical companies implement federated systems to achieve better prediction results and stronger teamwork and better protection for sensitive medical information and faster development of healthcare solutions in different clinical settings.

3.5.1. EXAM AI MODEL FOR COVID-19 PREDICTION

EXAM (EMR CXR AI Model) is a prime example of Federated Learning used in the context of prediction of COVID-19 in healthcare. In times of the pandemic, many hospitals have struggled to predict the disease prognosis and oxygen needs for patients due to lack of data exchange as a result of strict laws on personal privacy and urgency of joint efforts. In this respect, EXAM has managed to solve the problem, allowing for the simultaneous training of an AI model through Federated Learning without exchanging any personal data.

According to the described algorithm, all participating hospitals were able to train the model independently with their own dataset containing information about chest X-ray, lab tests, demographics, and vital signs. All that was exchanged between local devices and a central server consisted of only model updates and parameters that were aggregated through federated averaging to create a better global model. Privacy and data safety laws such as HIPAA and GDPR were respected throughout the process.

The EXAM model proved to be highly effective in predicting oxygen needs and severity of the disease in patients affected by COVID-19. The model was able to generalize better due to its ability to learn from data that were collected from different sources in various healthcare organizations. In conclusion, the EXAM project revealed the efficiency of Federated Learning in ensuring collaborative healthcare services in times of pandemic crises.

3.5.2. MOUNT SINAI FEDERATED EHR ANALYSIS

The Mount Sinai Federated EHR Analysis case study is an important example of the application of Federated Learning to conduct electronic health record (EHR) analysis. Patient information in EHRs includes diagnoses, lab results, medications, demographic information, treatment history, and many more, which are extremely useful for conducting research. However, such data cannot be shared outside an organization, as it may violate the privacy policy and other ethical norms of the organization. During the COVID-19 pandemic, Mount Sinai Health System in New York developed a Federated Learning model, allowing several hospitals from different organizations to engage in collaborative research without compromising data privacy.

For this study, five hospitals used their data sets consisting of patient demographics, medical history, lab results, and vital signs for training machine learning algorithms in their respective institutions. While they did not share any patient data, they sent their algorithms' learning information to a central server, where they were combined to develop a global predictive algorithm that analyzed various aspects of the patient's health status, such as risk of mortality and disease development.

Results proved that the federated learning approach yielded better prediction capabilities, especially in predicting mortality rates within 7 days of hospitalization for patients. On the whole, it was evident from the results that using the Federated Learning approach could greatly improve clinical decision making through healthcare data. Another achievement in this research proved the viability of collaboration among various hospitals while respecting patient privacy rights at the same time.

3.5.3. NVIDIA FLARE FOR MEDICAL IMAGING

AI model training needs extensive and varied datasets for medical imaging tasks which include tumor segmentation and disease classification and diagnostic analysis. Medical images require high security because they are stored at various locations which include hospitals and research centers and diagnostic laboratories.

NVIDIA created the NVIDIA FLARE (Federated Learning Application Runtime Environment) framework to solve these problems by providing a secure and scalable federated learning environment for healthcare and biomedical applications.

NVIDIA FLARE established a partnership with MONAI healthcare AI framework which allowed three medical institutions to conduct joint analysis of medical imaging data. The hospitals operated their own AI model development process using local imaging data while they sent encrypted model updates to the federated aggregation server.

The framework supported advanced privacy-preserving technologies including differential privacy, homomorphic encryption, and secure aggregation. NVIDIA FLARE powered multiple healthcare applications which included breast density classification pancreatic tumor segmentation brain tumor analysis and COVID-19 imaging studies.

The federated models developed using NVIDIA FLARE achieved performance levels comparable to centralized machine learning systems while maintaining patient confidentiality. The framework demonstrated that large-scale medical imaging collaborations could be achieved without directly sharing sensitive imaging datasets. NVIDIA FLARE also improved scalability and interoperability across healthcare institutions by providing standardized federated learning tools and workflow management systems. The success of the framework accelerated the adoption of FL in radiology, pathology, genomics, and biomedical imaging research.

3.5.4. MELLODDY PHARMACEUTICAL COLLABORATION

The process of drug discovery needs extensive chemical and biomedical data which makes it both expensive and data-driven. Pharmaceutical companies own important proprietary chemical collections and their research findings, yet they face barriers to collaboration because of their need to protect intellectual property and maintain data confidentiality while dealing with market competition.

The pharmaceutical industry established the MELLODDY project as its largest Federated Learning partnership to address these obstacles which multiple companies faced. The MELLODDY project enabled participating pharmaceutical organizations to collaboratively train AI models using millions of chemical compound records without exposing proprietary datasets. Each company trained machine learning models locally using its own chemical and biomedical data while sharing only model updates with the federated aggregation server. The federated architecture allowed organizations to benefit from collective learning while maintaining full control over confidential research data and intellectual property.

The MELLODDY project showed that Federated Learning technology speeded up drug discovery processes by enhancing prediction results and allowing AI systems to train on extensive chemical datasets which included various chemical compounds. The shared research framework which all partners used achieved better results for discovering novel candidates while it improved the performance of AI systems that supported pharmaceutical research activities.

The project demonstrated that organizations from different fields could work together safely by using machine learning systems which protected their privacy. The new system established a framework for pharmaceutical research and biomedical AI to drive cooperative research between organizations.

3.6. CHAPTER SUMMARY

In Chapter 3, an explanation is provided of what Federated Learning (FL) is and why it becomes increasingly popular among healthcare providers. The main focus is on the definition of Federated Learning as a distributed machine learning method that allows several organizations to train the same global model without collecting any personal information from their patients.

Next, a justification is made for Federated Learning implementation in healthcare because the data processed by hospitals and research facilities is extremely sensitive and includes electronic health records, medical images, and clinical data, for instance. Moreover, there is no need to store this data in one place since it poses a high risk and is subject to various regulations (e.g., HIPAA and GDPR).

An elaboration on the workflow of Federated Learning is provided. It starts with the process of initialization, proceeds with local training, and continues with global aggregation along with the iteration towards improving the performance of the model. The discussion also includes an overview of the architecture and a brief consideration of the communication framework, with emphasis on the key roles played by central servers, client nodes (hospitals and medical devices), communication security, and aggregation approaches such as Federated Averaging (FedAvg). An indispensable component of FL is the use of security techniques to protect sensitive information, including encryption, differential privacy, and secure aggregation.

In addition, this section provides an overview of the most prominent areas in which federated learning can be applied to the clinical data analysis. Specifically, these areas include medical imaging and diagnosis, EHR predictive analytics, drug discovery, clinical research, and monitoring of patients using IoMT technologies.

Multiple case studies are considered, including those involving EXAM AI's predictive system for detecting coronavirus, Mount Sinai's federated EHR analysis platform, NVIDIA FLARE for medical imaging, and MELLODDY's federated learning for discovering drugs. These examples demonstrate the efficiency of federated learning for collaborative work among multiple entities while preserving data privacy.

Lastly, the pros and cons of Federated Learning are discussed in this chapter. The strengths of Federated Learning include better data privacy, regulatory compliance, availability of varied data sets, lower data centralization, and collaboration, among others. However, there are some weaknesses associated with Federated Learning, such as communication overhead, heterogeneous data, security, synchronization problems, and complexity. Chapter 3 provides the conclusion that Federated Learning is a game-changing method for artificial intelligence models in the health care sector.

Multiple Choice Questions (MCQs)

1. **What is Federated Learning (FL)?**
   - A. A method of storing data in a single central server
   - B. A machine learning approach where data remains decentralized
   - C. A technique for encrypting healthcare data
   - D. A type of supervised learning algorithm
2. **In Federated Learning, where is the data primarily stored?**
   - A. On a central cloud server
   - B. On multiple distributed client devices or institutions
   - C. In public databases
   - D. On blockchain networks only
3. **What is the main goal of Federated Learning in healthcare?**
   - A. To increase data duplication
   - B. To improve model accuracy while preserving patient privacy
   - C. To eliminate machine learning models
   - D. To centralize all hospital data
4. **Which component coordinates the training process in a typical FL architecture?**
   - A. Local client nodes
   - B. Central aggregation server
   - C. Data warehouse
   - D. API gateway

5. **What is the role of local models in Federated Learning?**
   A. They replace the global model permanently
   B. They train on local data and share updates
   C. They store global datasets
   D. They act as backup systems
6. **Which of the following is a key application of FL in clinical data analysis?**
   A. Data deletion
   B. Disease prediction using distributed patient data
   C. Manual record keeping
   D. Hospital billing systems
7. **What is a major benefit of Federated Learning in healthcare?**
   A. Increased data sharing risks
   B. Reduced privacy
   C. Enhanced data security and privacy
   D. Slower computation speed
8. **Which of the following is a limitation of Federated Learning?**
   A. High communication overhead
   B. Lack of data availability
   C. No need for models
   D. Unlimited scalability
9. **In FL workflow, what happens after local training at client nodes?**
   A. Data is deleted
   B. Model updates are sent to the central server
   C. Data is shared publicly
   D. Training stops permanently

10. **Case studies in federated healthcare systems mainly demonstrate:**
    - A. Theoretical concepts only
    - B. Real-world implementation and effectiveness
    - C. Hardware design
    - D. Financial management strategies

Answers

1	2	3	4	5	6	7	8	9	10
B	B	B	B	B	B	C	A	B	B

Chapter 4

CRYPTOGRAPHIC APPROACHES IN AI

4.1. HOMOMORPHIC ENCRYPTION IN HEALTHCARE AI

The adoption of"artificial intelligence"(AI) at lightning speed in healthcare systems offers significant potentials in decision making, mobile diagnostics, and population-level analytics. However, the integration of AI also opens up new risks relating to cybersecurity including data-in-use leaks, sensitive record reconstruction, and federated learning. The protection of these extremely sensitive medical data streams from these kinds of risks remains an important issue given the shift in computation towards resource-constrained and distributed computing paradigms, such as wearable sensors, telemedicine tools, and edge computing devices.

"Homomorphic encryption" (HE) serves as one of the most basic concepts when it comes to the application of privacy-preserving techniques in AI technologies. Data confidentiality in certain applications like healthcare, finance, and smart sensing is a critical requirement for privacy-preserving machine learning. AI operations are also conducted using distributed systems including wearable devices and cloud-based infrastructure. Due to the increasing usage of distributed AI systems, there has been increased risk of data leakage in training, inference, and data transfer processes. Recent studies have revealed that the combination of cybersecurity and AI technologies has evolved into a system-level paradigm focused on real-time threat detection and resilience.

4.1.1. HOMOMORPHIC ENCRYPTION APPLICATIONS IN HEALTHCARE AI

Homomorphic encryption is an important technique that is applied in the healthcare domain for the purpose of safeguarding the confidentiality of health analytics that are conducted using artificial intelligence algorithms, where computations can be performed on the ciphertext directly without any need for decrypting patient data.

- **Safe Healthcare Computation Outsourcing:** It is safe for healthcare firms to entrust cloud infrastructure with computation because homomorphic encryption ensures that the private patient information is not revealed. The process of medical data analysis and prediction using cryptography can therefore be done within healthcare organizations without compromising patient privacy. For example, hospitals and other institutions can analyze encrypted EHR stored in clouds without revealing patient information.
- **Healthcare Data Analytics That Preserve Privacy:** While protecting data privacy, homomorphic encryption enables safe analysis of encrypted medical datasets. Since sensitive data about patients has to be kept confidential, this tool is particularly helpful in medical research, epidemiological studies, and disease prediction. Since there is a possibility of leaking sensitive data illegally, this problem could be addressed using statistical analysis and healthcare analytics based on AI without the necessity of decrypting data.
- **Healthcare AI using Confidential Machine Learning:** For learning and predictions, many machine learning algorithms in the healthcare sector require large amounts of data. Using homomorphic encryption, various healthcare organizations can collaborate to develop machine learning algorithms without the need for sharing any sensitive patient data. This ensures that federated learning is secure in areas such as cancer prediction, medical image processing, and clinical decision-making tools.

- **Safe Exchange and Cooperation of Medical Data:** Protected medical data can be securely exchanged by healthcare institutions, research institutions, and healthcare professionals through homomorphic encryption. The transmission of encrypted datasets and computation by these institutions on the encrypted dataset takes place in a manner that does not breach any private information compared to the transmission of non-encrypted patient information.

In conclusion, homomorphic encryption plays a critical role in ensuring the safety of health data that undergoes analysis through AI technology for purposes of securing computations, performing private analysis, implementing secure machine learning, and sharing of health information.

4.1.2. HOMOMORPHIC ENCRYPTION TECHNIQUES AND SCHEMES

In HE, there is no requirement for the process of decrypting data in order to perform computations on them. Due to this characteristic of HE, its significance becomes apparent in healthcare AI technologies wherein it is essential to preserve the confidentiality of the patient's information including genetic databases, medical images, and electronic health records. HE is useful in developing machine learning technologies aimed at ensuring privacy and securing medical analysis.

- **Partially Homomorphic Encryption (PHE):** The use of partially homomorphic encryption enables only one mathematical function, such as addition or multiplication, to be conducted on the encrypted data. This method is recommended for resource-limited health care environments and lightweight medical systems that require only limited encryption computations.
- **Somewhat Homomorphic Encryption (SHE):** Addition and multiplication can be performed via somewhat homomorphic encryption, yet only up to a limited number of computations before decryption becomes necessary. SHE is typically employed in statistics computation in ciphertext form, as well

as basic healthcare machine learning operations requiring computational depth.

- **Performance and Computational Challenges:** However, while offering very good security, homomorphic encryption methods incur considerable costs in terms of computation time. Fully Homomorphic Encryption might be much slower than processing the same information unencrypted, while encrypted data may consume more space and communication channel throughput. This creates difficulties when implementing AI solutions in healthcare settings that require low latency.

Homomorphic encryption is very crucial in ensuring that health care information remains confidential while supporting the use of artificial intelligence in the analysis of such data. Various techniques have been used to ensure that health care data can be processed using various levels of homomorphic encryption. Despite the challenges posed by computational complexity and latency, homomorphic encryption techniques continue to improve.

4.2. SECURE MULTI-PARTY COMPUTATION (SMPC)

Over the past few decades, data security and privacy have become everyone's top concerns. With the development of the internet and technology, data security and privacy in distributed networks have grown to be key concerns. Secure Multiparty Computation (SMPC) offers a workable solution to this issue by allowing partners to compute a function on their private inputs without revealing them to outside parties.

Parties can safely compute a function jointly without revealing each other's distinct inputs by using the cryptographic technique known as "secure multiparty computation." This allows for computations and analysis while protecting data privacy. SMPC is utilised when privacy is crucial, such as in financial transactions, healthcare data, or personal information transferred between several institutions (Rahaman et al., 2024).

4.2.1. ARCHITECTURE AND TECHNIQUES OF SECURE MULTI-PARTY COMPUTATION

Secure Multi-Party Computation Architecture is an architectural framework aimed at allowing a group of people to work together in performing computations involving sensitive information without disclosing any part of that information among themselves. The architecture makes use of cryptographic techniques to keep information confidential and protected from being exposed. In the architecture, participants have access to their private information while participating in computations.

The main components that make up SMPC architecture include the participants' data inputs, the computation process by which computations are done, the secure communication channel for exchanging information, cryptography for protection of information, and results obtained from computations. Participants' data inputs are kept confidential before being processed into an output after computations have been performed.

Several cryptographic methods are employed within Secure Multi-Party Computation architecture in order to protect sensitive information throughout the entire process. Cryptography helps in keeping the computation process secure, protecting information when it is stored and communicated. Different cryptography methods are employed depending on the type of computation to be carried out.

The various methods used in Secure Multi-party Computation (SMPC) allow for secure computation in a multi-party setting. They ensure that the involved participants collaborate in their computations while ensuring privacy and security of their data.

- **Secret Sharing:** The secret sharing method involves splitting the sensitive information into several shares. The original data can only be recovered by putting all the relevant shares together.
- **Garbled Circuits:** Garbled circuits are mainly used in secure authentication and machine learning. The technique allows

the evaluation of the function without exposing any private input.

- **Homomorphic Encryption:** This is an important encryption technique since it allows computations on data that have been encrypted without decrypting the same.
- **Oblivious Transfer:** It is a privacy protocol that allows the involved participants to transfer information securely while maintaining their privacy.
- **Zero Knowledge Proofs:** With the help of this technique, one participant is allowed to verify the data without revealing the actual data. This method is frequently used in authentication and also in blockchain technology for security purposes.
- **Threshold Cryptography:** For the decryption process, all the participants must work together. By doing so, security can be improved by avoiding any unauthorized access.
- **Secure Aggregation**: In secure aggregation, the aggregation process takes place of data that is encrypted by different individuals at the same time. It is widely applied in federated learning and artificial intelligence frameworks as well.

To conclude, the design of SMPC framework provides a safe platform that facilitates collaborative computation without compromising the privacy of the data involved. SMPC uses cryptographic approaches to ensure privacy, including secret sharing, garbled circuits, homomorphic encryption, and secure aggregation. Thus, SMPC can be widely adopted in healthcare, banking, cloud computing, and artificial intelligence.

4.2.2. BENEFITS AND LIMITATIONS OF SECURE MULTIPARTY COMPUTATION

The term SMPC refers to Secure Multi-party Computation. It is a powerful cryptographic approach which enables several parties to engage in computing without revealing their sensitive information. This process provides high levels of security and privacy while processing data in a distributed networking environment. The SMPC technique can be applied in fields such as health care, banking, cloud computing, cyber-security, and AI where privacy and collaboration are required. However, there are some drawbacks to this technique as well.

- **Benefits of Secure Multiparty Computation**

  First and foremost, the ability to preserve data privacy is one of the main advantages associated with SMPC. The technology enables users to collaborate in analysing data using several sets of information without sharing the original data. In this way, data confidentiality can be maintained and private data can be protected from illegal access.

  Secure cooperation is another important characteristic of SMPC that enables companies and individuals to cooperate in order to work with private data. For example, several healthcare institutions can collaborate in analysing patient records and conducting medical research while keeping data safe from illegal access.

  Moreover, SMPC is effective for decreasing the probability of data leaks due to the absence of the actual data transfer and storage. Therefore, there is a low risk of cyber-attacks, data leaks, and other issues associated with information privacy.

  Furthermore, it is easier for companies to ensure compliance with certain laws associated with data confidentiality through the use of SMPC. Moreover, the technology is beneficial in developing distributed artificial intelligence systems.

- **Challenges Faced by Secure Multi-Party Computation**

  As promising as it is, there are some limitations of using Secure Multi-Party Computation. First, SMPC entails a high degree of computational complexity. The protocols in use are highly complex in terms of their cryptography, making them relatively slow compared to the traditional computation approach.

  SMPC also has considerable communication overhead. SMPC typically uses many iterations of communication to reach a consensus among all parties involved. While that may not be a problem in some cases, in others, such iterations can make SMPC quite inefficient in its operation.

Thirdly, it can be slower in performing computations. Computations using encryption or secret sharing are often more resource-intensive than regular computation processes. It means that real-time applications will likely encounter difficulties with the delay in the process due to its complexity.

Finally, SMPC can also pose a challenge in its implementation and maintenance. To design and implement an effective SMPC system, you need a high level of understanding of cryptography, distributed systems, and secure communications. Furthermore, scaling becomes a bit of an issue with increased numbers of participants or data volumes (Sahai, 2013).

4.3. PRIVACY-PRESERVING MODEL TRAINING

Rapid growth in the application of machine learning has significantly impacted how firms utilize data analytics, extract meaningful patterns, and automate complex processes. Machine learning models are being applied by industries such as healthcare, financial services, cybersecurity, and others to obtain meaningful insights from big data. Nonetheless, the increasing use of sensitive data in training models has become a big cause for concern with respect to data privacy and security.

The technique of creating machine learning models without jeopardising the privacy of the data used in the process is known as "privacy-preserving training of models." There are significant hazards associated with centralised data collecting, including data leaks and attack vulnerabilities that could reveal private information. For this reason, different measures aimed at ensuring privacy when training machine learning models have been employed.

Federated learning, differential privacy, homomorphic encryption, and SMPC are a few significant privacy-preserving strategies. In industries including healthcare, finance, and cloud computing, privacy-preserving machine learning models are necessary because protecting sensitive information becomes critical. While difficulties like additional computing cost and reduced performance persist, developments in AI and cryptography are making privacy-preserving models more efficient and secure.

4.3.1. KEY TECHNIQUES FOR PRIVACY-PRESERVING MACHINE LEARNING

There are several methods that are employed in machine learning that protects privacy to ensure data security in the processes of data acquisition, processing, and machine learning model development. These methods allow developing machine learning algorithms that can protect sensitive data privacy when working with it. Such methods find wide application in areas like healthcare, finance, cybersecurity, cloud computing, and AI where data security is critically important for organizations.

Some techniques employed in privacy-preserving machine learning include:

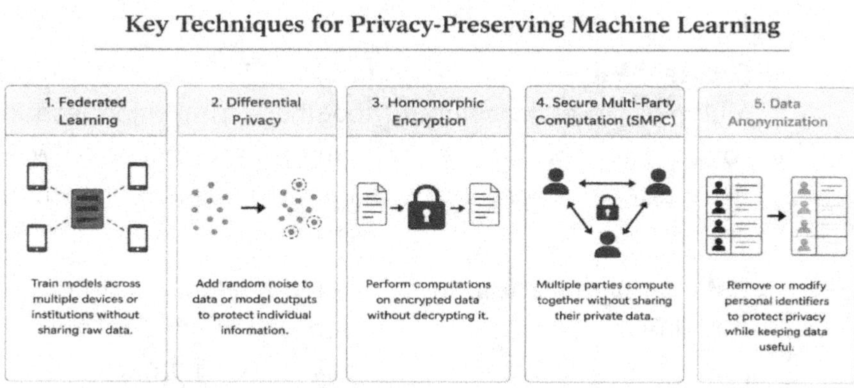

Figure 4.1: Key Techniques for Privacy-Preserving Machine Learning

Source: (Author 2026)

Key Techniques for Privacy-Preserving Machine Learning

As shown in Figure 4.1 below, the main techniques that can be utilized in privacy-preserving machine learning to safeguard sensitive data while training AI models are discussed here.

- **Federated Learning:** In federated learning, various devices or institutions can jointly train machine learning algorithms without exchanging their data in plain form. Model parameters or updates alone are shared between the parties involved in such a process, hence preserving privacy and minimizing risks of data leaks.
- **Differential Privacy:** The concept of differential privacy entails protection of personal details via addition of random noise into either the dataset itself or its model output. This way, there is no possibility for data points to be identified.
- **Homomorphic Encryption:** Through homomorphic encryption, operations on data can be performed in their encrypted form without being decrypted first, thus ensuring data remains confidential.
- **Secure Multi-Party Computation (SMPC):** SMPC allows multiple parties to compute together on machine learning computations without sharing any private details between themselves. This approach is useful when collaborating among organizations working with sensitive data.
- **Data Anonymization:** In this method, sensitive information contained within data is removed or modified in order to prevent the breach of privacy while keeping the data usable. This is typically practiced in the healthcare industry.

Privacy-preserving machine learning techniques offer safe ways of handling sensitive data during the training procedure for machine learning algorithms. This covers methods for data anonymization, secure multi-party computation, homomorphic encryption, federated learning, and differential privacy. They are essential for improving the security, confidentiality, and dependability of the existing machine learning models (Kim & Tanuwidjaja, 2021).

4.3.2. PRACTICAL APPLICATIONS OF PRIVACY-PRESERVING MODEL TRAINING

Privacy-preserving techniques for model training have become popular in many applications in which privacy has to be maintained when using machine learning and artificial intelligence. In other words, such techniques make it possible to create an accurate and effective AI model while ensuring that sensitive data is protected from any access and any potential leakages that can happen as a result of cyberattacks.

Examples of practical usage of privacy-preserving machine learning training are as follows:

- **Applications in Healthcare:** In hospitals and other medical organizations, privacy-preserving machine learning is used for predictions regarding health issues, analysis of medical images, monitoring of patients, and making decisions based on clinical systems. The technologies help conduct collaborative research in medicine without disclosing private medical data.
- **Application in Finance:** Financial companies utilize safe machine learning algorithms to detect frauds, monitor transactions, analyze customers' behaviors, and calculate risks without exposing confidential information about customers.
- **Cyber Security Systems:** Privacy-preserving tools enable the detection of malware, phishing, cyber-attacks, and unusual activity within a network while protecting the confidentiality of the data from any individual or organization. They enhance the monitoring and security of cybersecurity threats.
- **Cloud Computing:** Organizations are able to process and analyses the encrypted data through cloud computing by adopting privacy-preserving tools like homomorphic encryption and secure multi-party computation that mitigate the risks related to centralized cloud processing.

- **Smart Devices and IoT:** Federated learning allow smart devices and IoT to learn and collaborate to build a machine learning model without disclosing sensitive user information to central servers.

Privacy-preserving training of models is vital in ensuring secure and dependable AI applications in different industries. Since such technologies allow companies to protect sensitive data during the process of machine learning, they contribute to the achievement of safe cooperation, improved security, and data privacy. Privacy-preserving techniques are becoming more crucial as AI is widely used in a variety of industries, including healthcare, banking, cybersecurity, cloud computing, and smart devices (Kim & Tanuwidjaja, 2021).

4.3.3. CHALLENGES AND FUTURE DIRECTIONS

There are many advantages related to privacy-preserving methods for machine learning models, but there are certain technical obstacles as well. One of the main obstacles is computational complexity, Techniques that protect privacy, like safe multi-party computation and homomorphic encryption involve heavy computations that require powerful computer hardware.

Furthermore, there is a problem with communication due to the need for exchange of information in distributed networks. For instance, in federated learning, there must be a trade-off between privacy preservation and the performance of the algorithm. There could be other barriers involving certain skill sets and security frameworks.

Nonetheless, modern developments in artificial intelligence, cryptography, and cloud computing have significantly boosted the capacity of privacy-preserving machine learning technologies. Future developments would likely be geared toward lowering computational costs, boosting performance, enhancing real-time applications, and safeguarding data better.

4.4. PERFORMANCE AND SCALABILITY CONSIDERATIONS

Performance and scalability are important issues that must be considered in privacy-preserving AI and ML models. In most cases, cryptographic algorithms such as homomorphic encryption, federated learning, and secure multiparty computations usually require high computing power, memory requirements, and bandwidth utilization.

Scaling is difficult in distributed settings where the number of participants, devices, or datasets grows. Scalable AI platforms might be subjected to elevated latency, communication costs, and storage demands while training the secure model and processing the data.

Optimized algorithms, lighter cryptographic protocols, and efficient distributed computing systems are some of the approaches used to overcome these difficulties. Enhanced performance and scalability are crucial for implementing privacy-preserving AI solutions in health care, finance, cloud computing, and IoT applications (Liu, 2011).

4.4.1. SCALABILITY ACROSS LARGE DATASETS AND COMPLEX AI MODELS

Privacy-preserving artificial intelligence systems are increasingly required to process massive datasets and support highly complex machine learning models. In fields such as health care, finance, and cybersecurity, AI applications often involve millions of records, high-dimensional features, and deep neural networks with millions of parameters. When cryptographic techniques such as HE, SMPC, and Differential Privacy are integrated into these systems, computational demands increase substantially.

Homomorphic encryption performs arithmetic directly on encrypted data, but ciphertexts are significantly larger than plaintext values and require expensive polynomial computations. In the same vein, the Secure Multi-Party Computation protocol requires several rounds of communication between different parties in each computation phase. As the amount of data and model complexity grows, the volume of encrypted computations and communications also increases exponentially, impacting runtime and resource consumption.

However, despite these obstacles, privacy-preserving machine learning can still be scaled successfully through enhanced encryption algorithms, efficient software architecture, and distributed computing frameworks. Batching, parallelization, and compression methods allow for applying cryptography on big data machine learning tasks without compromising computational efficiency (Mishra, 2024).

4.4.2. COMPUTATIONAL OVERHEAD AND LATENCY

Encryption, decryption, key generation, and secure computations all lead to increased computational cost relative to the usual machine learning process. Fully Homomorphic Encryption may take significantly longer to compute than ordinary computations in plaintext

The issue of latency is especially relevant in real-time applications such as clinical decision-making, fraud detection, and self-driving vehicles. Latency can be an issue in Secure Multiparty Computation due to repeated communication cycles that can occur when performing multiplications and comparisons. The same applies to Differential Privacy in relation to clipping the gradients and adding noise to the training data.

Efforts must be made to minimize latency through algorithmic and hardware solutions such as GPU computing, vectorization, and approximate algorithms such as CKKS.

4.4.3. MEMORY, STORAGE, AND COMMUNICATION REQUIREMENTS

It must be admitted that the utilization of AI algorithms featuring data privacypreservationrequirestheapplicationofmoreresourcesconcerning memory, storage, and computational power than conventional machine learning frameworks do. The key factors contributing to this trend are related to the use of cryptography-based methods and distribution-based learning frameworks that bring additional overhead.

An increase in memory requirements occurs due to the need to compute the values of operations in an encrypted format and utilize cryptographical techniques. This factor becomes especially significant for deep learning frameworks since there are millions of parameters needed to be computed during both training and inference procedures.

An increase in storage requirements takes place owing to the larger sizes of encrypted data created through the utilization of cryptography-based algorithms like Homomorphic Encryption and Secure Multi-Party Computation. Consequently, higher storage is required for the purpose of keeping encrypted datasets, models and output.

In turn, communication overhead is a major issue for distributed learning solutions including Federated Learning. In particular, regular exchanges between the participants of the process and transfer of the encrypted model updates causes higher overhead in terms of communication. Efforts are currently made to optimize privacy-preserving AI systems through the development of model compression techniques and efficient encryption methods.

4.4.4. OPTIMIZATION STRATEGIES FOR SCALABILITY

A number of optimization methods are applied to enhance the scalability and performance of privacy-preserving AI solutions. The goal of such optimizations is to minimize computation costs, minimize communication overhead, reduce memory footprint while ensuring high-levels of data security and privacy.

One of the main methods used in homomorphic encryption is ciphertext batching. This approach involves packing several values into a single cipher and processing them at once. This method helps to increase the computation speed and capacity of the algorithms significantly. Approximate encryption such as CKKS allows performing machine learning computations on real numbers securely.

Another crucial component of enhancing scalability in this domain is the use of parallel and distributed computation approaches that distribute the encrypted tasks between multiple processors, GPUs, or cloud machines. This allows reducing the overall processing time and conducting large-scale computations securely. Hardware acceleration through GPUs and FPGA is used to boost computational speed.

Moreover, optimization approaches for machine learning models, including pruning, quantization, and knowledge distillation, allow achieving smaller model sizes and lower computational costs. As a result, fewer cryptography calculations will be performed during the training process and the execution phase. On the whole, all of these optimization methods contribute to improving the efficiency of privacy-preserving AI solutions (Pelikan et al., 2006).

4.5. CHAPTER SUMMARY

This chapter provided an in-depth conversation on cryptographic methods for AI by concentrating on privacy-preserving technologies. The chapter started with homomorphic encryption in health care AI, which explains that encrypted calculations can be performed using the method in order to do secure computation, collaborative machine learning, and privacy-preserving health care applications. Various methods of homomorphic encryption, including somewhat and partially homomorphic encryption, were described along with the computation difficulties involved. Further, this chapter provided information about SMPC along with its architecture, cryptographic methods used, advantages, and disadvantages.

Techniques for private model training were also covered, particularly concentrating on the critical methods combining homomorphic encryption, differential privacy, and federated learning, and SMPC. The chapter explored how these methods were applied practically in various industries, such as medicine, finance, cybersecurity, cloud services, and IoT technology, noting the necessity for securing the creation of AI models.

Lastly, performance and scalability were also assessed in relation to issues relating to computational cost, latency, memory requirements, data storage, and communication requirements. Techniques for improving on these factors included ciphertext batching, parallel processing, model compression, and hardware acceleration. Therefore, in this chapter, it was found that although cryptography poses some challenges related to performance, it is crucial to ensuring that AI functions properly.

Multiple Choice Questions (MCQs)

1. **What is the primary purpose of homomorphic encryption in healthcare AI?**
   A. To increase model accuracy
   B. To allow computation on encrypted data without decryption
   C. To reduce storage requirements
   D. To speed up training time

2. **Which type of homomorphic encryption supports arbitrary computations on ciphertexts?**
   A. Partial Homomorphic Encryption
   B. Somewhat Homomorphic Encryption
   C. Fully Homomorphic Encryption
   D. Symmetric Encryption

3. **In healthcare AI, homomorphic encryption is mainly used to:**
   A. Visualize patient data
   B. Share data publicly
   C. Protect sensitive patient information during processing
   D. Replace machine learning models

4. **What does Secure Multi-Party Computation (SMPC) enable?**
   A. One party to control all computations
   B. Multiple parties to jointly compute a function without revealing their inputs
   C. Faster computation using GPUs
   D. Data compression across networks

5. **Which of the following is a key advantage of SMPC?**
   A. Eliminates need for encryption
   B. Ensures data privacy among multiple participants
   C. Reduces algorithm complexity
   D. Increases data redundancy
6. **Privacy-preserving model training primarily aims to:**
   A. Improve visualization techniques
   B. Prevent data leakage during model training
   C. Increase dataset size
   D. Simplify algorithms
7. **Which technique is commonly used for privacy-preserving AI training?**
   A. Differential Privacy
   B. Linear Regression
   C. Data Mining
   D. Clustering
8. **What is a major challenge of homomorphic encryption?**
   A. Lack of security
   B. High computational overhead
   C. Inability to encrypt data
   D. Limited applications
9. **In SMPC, data is typically:**
   A. Shared openly among all parties
   B. Encrypted or split into secret shares
   C. Stored in a central database
   D. Deleted after computation

10. **Performance and scalability in cryptographic AI systems are affected by:**
    A. Only hardware quality
    B. Encryption techniques and computational complexity
    C. User interface design
    D. Data visualization tools

Answers

1	2	3	4	5	6	7	8	9	10
B	C	C	B	B	B	A	B	B	B

Chapter 5

PRIVACY IN CLINICAL DATA AND EHR SYSTEMS

5.1. STRUCTURE OF ELECTRONIC HEALTH RECORDS (EHR)

A person's whole medical history, including diseases, surgeries, treatments, prescriptions, immunizations, vitals, and much more, can be documented in an electronic health record. In addition to serving as constant digital assistants, next-generation EHRs will automate a number of clinicians' tedious duties, like scheduling visits, taking notes, and managing referrals, freeing them up to concentrate on building relationships with patients and making wise judgements. EHRs also give clinicians access to information and context that they may have overlooked with a more compartmentalized record system by gathering patient data from providers across the healthcare ecosystem, regardless of where treatment was received. For a thorough examination, continue reading.

Digital health records that collect, store, and arrange patient data using standardized formats are referred to as structured "Electronic Health Records" (EHRs). In contrast to conventional, unstructured paper records, structured electronic health records (EHRs) rely on established fields, data points, and codes to guarantee that patient data is arranged consistently, conveniently, and analytically. Improved data accuracy, effective clinical decision-making, and simplified information sharing among healthcare providers are all made possible by this arrangement (Sinha et al., 2012).

5.1.1. WHAT IS AN EHR IN HEALTHCARE

Digital copies of a patient's medical history, including diagnoses, treatment plans, test results, surgical procedures, and lifestyle markers like drug, alcohol, and smoking behaviour, are stored and managed by electronic health records (EHRs). Additionally, they display visit records, prescriptions, and recommendations. They can also establish connections with other providers to obtain patient information from locations other than the patient's regular treatment center. The most up-to-date EHRs offer visualization tools to highlight pertinent, useful information that doctors may utilize to promote precise diagnosis and improved treatment choices.

Advances in AI technology, changing interoperability standards, and new methods for providers to interact with digital systems—like chatbots and voice commands—will all help next-generation EHRs. Clinicians will be able to use EHRs to do more than just order tests and medications, manually code diagnoses, and enter scanned documents. Instead, they will be able to automate manual workflows, create individualised treatment plans based on nearly real-time data, promote teamwork, and learn how patients' lifestyles and living standards may influence their care.

5.1.2. BENEFITS OF EHRS

There are many benefits that can be derived from the implementation of EHRs. The innovations in EHRs are aiding the healthcare professionals in managing their daily tasks more efficiently and offering informed treatment to patients. Some of the important benefits of using EHRs are described below:

- Enhanced patient care and safety.
- Streamlined workflows and enhanced efficiencies.
- Optimized coordination among providers.

- Limited paperwork and administrative costs.
- Enhanced data security and privacy.
- Easy access to patient health history.
- Support for data-driven decision-making and research.

Electronic Health Records have revolutionized healthcare in contemporary times by facilitating efficient, accurate, accessible, and secure management of patient data. The use of EHRs makes healthcare more effective by enabling informed decision making, fostering collaboration between practitioners, decreasing paperwork, and improving patient safety.

Moreover, EHRs are crucial for ensuring regulatory compliance, securing sensitive patient data, and conducting research studies within the field of medicine. With further advancements in healthcare technology, EHRs are predicted to become increasingly sophisticated and indispensable for providing superior patient care.

5.1.3. TYPES OF EHR IMPLEMENTATIONS

There are various deployment methods for implementing Electronic Health Records (EHR). The deployment method be contingent on several factors including the size of the organization, the needs of the organization, budget, and technological capability among others. There are mainly two ways of implementing Electronic Health Records. These include on-premise EHR and cloud-based EHR.

- **On- Premises EHR Systems:** On-site EHR systems are systems that are installed and run within the facility by utilizing servers and IT systems on-site. The hospitals or clinics are responsible for managing and updating these systems as well as ensuring their safety and maintaining data storage. These systems provide more security and control but come at a higher cost and need for IT support.
- **Cloud-Based EHR Systems:** Cloud-based EHR systems are those that operate using remote servers connected via the

internet. These systems help in eliminating the need for IT infrastructure, are easier to manage and maintain, and enable remote accessibility and easy communication between healthcare professionals.

- **Hybrid EHR Systems:** Hybrid EHR systems are a combination of both on-site and cloud-based systems where some services are provided through cloud computing while others are performed locally.

It can be concluded that various EHR implementation models come with unique benefits. The on-premise model is more secure and gives the organization greater control, whereas the cloud model is more flexible and cost-effective. The hybrid approach combines all the strengths of the two models. The organization selects an appropriate EHR implementation model according to its specific needs (Pereira, 2025).

5.1.4. EHR DEPLOYMENT CHALLENGES

EHR installations can be difficult and complicated initiatives with significant financial and operational ramifications. Healthcare providers may experience resistance to change, data transfer problems, and cost overruns in the absence of adequate planning and user training. When preparing for a deployment, keep the following things in mind:

- **Implementation costs.** In addition to software license, hardware, and IT personnel costs for on-premises systems or per-user fees for cloud-based systems, the costs of implementing an EHR include training. EHR systems must adapt to evolving regulatory, auditing, and interoperability requirements to ensure secure and efficient healthcare data exchange.
- **Training and user adoption**. Training programs that are tailored for certain roles, engage trainees, and consider the time constraints of physicians are necessary to promote the adoption of an EHR. Additionally, clinicians' comfort level with

the EHR and the quality of their training must be continuously assessed by providers.

- **Data migration and integration.** It might be challenging to transfer data from an old EHR to a new one. Open standards-based EHRs reduce operational disruption and make data movement easier.
- **System interoperability.** It was challenging to obtain a comprehensive, accurate, and current perspective of a patient's history because the first electronic records were compartmentalized and limited to a particular practice or facility. One of the largest hurdles in the healthcare industry is developing EHRs that are patient-centric, which means that all patient data is combined into a single view, as opposed to provider-centric.
- **Transition downtime**. Any unscheduled EHR outage during the switch to a new system might endanger patient safety, result in lost income, and raise labor costs because of the extra overtime compensation and staff time needed to update offline records. By testing updates in a virtual environment and selecting low-impact times to finish live upgrades, organizations can reduce this risk.
- **Compliance.** Healthcare regulations and standards often evolve rapidly, presenting significant challenges in terms of compliance. Electronic health records must be able to accommodate the evolving regulatory environment, auditing, and interoperability needs for secure and efficient data exchange among different healthcare environments.

From the above discussion, there are various difficulties associated with implementing an EHR system in healthcare organizations. Effective planning, staff training, data migration security, interoperability, and compliance with regulations are some of the important factors necessary for effective EHR adoption. Overcoming these difficulties ensures more efficient and secure handling of patient records and provision of better healthcare services.

5.1.5. KEY FUNCTIONS OF EHRS

By automating procedures, providing point-of-care insights, streamlining patient intake, documentation, and clinical follow-up, and assisting with regulatory compliance, EHRs are made to handle the complete clinical workflow. Continue reading to learn more about these and other features.

1. **Storing and managing patient health data**. EHRs provide doctors with the context they need to determine the best course of action by storing and managing patient medication, medical history, and other data gathered over time. Anonymized patient data is used by researchers to create clinical trial procedures and identify trial participants, while public health officials utilize it to monitor disease and illness incidents.
2. **Facilitating electronic prescriptions.** The electronic order input features of EHRs can simplify the ordering of tests and prescriptions while lowering errors and identifying potentially harmful drug interactions.
3. **Scheduling and managing appointments**. EHRs can be integrated with appointment scheduling and management software, allowing desk workers to concentrate on higher-level tasks. By offering a perspective of forthcoming appointments, the purpose of each patient's visit, and an overview of their medical records, they can also assist doctors in planning their day.
4. **Tracking patient progress and medical history.** In order to provide doctors with context for future diagnoses and treatments, electronic health records (EHRs) compile a comprehensive, longitudinal record of a patient's medical history, including diagnoses, treatments, procedures, prescriptions, and lifestyle markers. Through voice dictation and standardized templates that may be tailored for specialty workflows, these records assist physicians in properly and effectively recording the specifics of clinical encounters.

5. **Enabling clinical decision support.** The most recent EHRs can improve clinical decision-making by delivering the appropriate data at the appropriate moment. New forms of user interfaces, such as voice, text, and guided workflows, have made it possible for doctors to access extensive patient and third-party diagnostic data, including government health data, drug catalogs, and clinical trial results.
6. **Supporting billing and coding**. In order to automate coding and expedite payer reimbursement, a provider's finance team can retrieve pertinent data from a patient's record and forward it to billing and revenue management. Coding mistakes that could lead to claim denials are less likely to occur in streamlined operations.
7. **Enhancing communication between providers.** EHRs enhance communication between healthcare professionals by standardizing data formats and using interoperable systems. EHRs are also useful in managing referrals and facilitating access to patient data from multiple healthcare institutions.

Immediately, the EHR system is responsible for executing many critical tasks that make the delivery of healthcare more efficient and effective. Some of these tasks include handling patients' medical records and prescribing drugs electronically. In addition, EHRs facilitate the decision-making process and foster communication between healthcare professionals.

5.2. DATA SHARING AND INTEROPERABILITY CHALLENGES

While healthcare organizations recognize the importance of interoperability and efficient data sharing, several barriers continue to hinder the implementation of interoperable systems. These challenges affect technical integration, data quality, security, governance, financial sustainability, and user adoption. The major interoperability challenges in healthcare are discussed below.

Challenges of Interoperability in Healthcare

Despite the fact that many healthcare providers recognize the value of interoperability and the necessity of achieving every level, there are substantial obstacles that may make it difficult to make decisions on the establishment of an interoperable system.

1. The following are the main obstacles to interoperability in the healthcare industry:
2. System fragmentation and technical obstacles
3. Semantic Gaps and Data Quality
4. Risks to Privacy, Security, and Compliance
5. Policy and Governance Obstacles
6. Budgetary and Resource Limitations
7. Adoption and Cultural Difficulties

To conclude, even though interoperability and data sharing provide many advantages for healthcare delivery and patients' health needs, there remain a number of barriers that prevent the successful application of these concepts. Overcoming these barriers by implementing appropriate technologies and taking necessary steps will contribute greatly to the improvement of healthcare collaborations.

5.2.1. TECHNICAL BARRIERS AND SYSTEM FRAGMENTATION

One of the problems with achieving interoperability in healthcare is the existence of technical barriers and the fragmentation of healthcare systems. The EHR systems, software, and databases utilized by various healthcare entities might not necessarily be compatible with each other. Because the technology used to create these systems differs from one vendor to another and follows different technical standards, it can be difficult to share patient data.

There are many health institutions that rely on their own legacy systems that do not have interoperable capabilities. Legacy systems may not have modern capabilities such as application programming interfaces (APIs), HL7, or FHIR standards, which are required for transferring data across various systems.

Some of the major technical challenges faced include:

- Lack of uniform healthcare infrastructure
- Discrepancy between different software programs and databases
- Over-reliance on old legacy IT systems
- Difficulties in combining many healthcare technologies together
- Limited interoperability

Healthcare system fragmentation causes delays in accessing patients' information, duplicity of medical tests, ineffective collaboration among healthcare providers, and higher risk of medical mistakes. Therefore, it is necessary for healthcare organizations to use standardized and interoperable technologies.

5.2.2. DATA QUALITY AND SEMANTIC GAPS

Successful healthcare interoperability relies heavily on data quality, consistency, and precision in terms of healthcare data. Badly maintained data quality results in unreliable EHRs and poor patient care and decision-making. Data quality problems can be described by such examples as incomplete patient records, duplication of data, inaccuracies, improper format usage, or even human error when entering data.

Semantically inconsistent health data is another problem for healthcare organizations. There are different coding systems and data standards that different healthcare organizations use to store patient information. As an illustration, some systems may use ICD-10 coding while other organizations have different codes or abbreviations for the same diagnosis.

The problem of semantic discrepancies could negatively affect the process of communication between healthcare providers and pose threats to patient safety due to misinterpretation of information related to medications, allergic conditions, lab results, and diagnostics. Moreover, relevant clinical information might be lost during the transition of healthcare data from one system to another, which would make it hard for physicians to diagnose patients' health problems correctly. In order to deal with these problems, standardized terminology in the healthcare industry needs to be implemented. Effective communication and interoperability in the field of healthcare depend on it.

5.2.3. PRIVACY, SECURITY, AND COMPLIANCE RISKS

There are serious issues related to privacy, security, and compliance that need to be considered before using healthcare data interoperability services. The Electronic Health Records store very sensitive patient information, including health history, diagnostic results, medical treatments, insurance details, and patient identification. The protection of data, together with preventing any unauthorized usage and disclosures, is an important aspect of the functioning of the healthcare institution.

The more healthcare institutions become integrated, the more the possibility of their being penetrated emerges. Hackers tend to get into electronic databases in order to steal private data. The main threats in cybersecurity for the healthcare industry include ransomware attacks, phishing, malware, insider attacks, or any other kind of penetration into patients' databases.

The healthcare sector uses a number of methods, such as firewalls, access control policies, multi-factor authentication, encryption, and audits, to safeguard patient-sensitive information. Besides the technology involved, healthcare institutions should also follow certain data privacy and protection policies. The HIPAA and GDPR policies provide clear guidelines regarding how to deal with patients' data. Non-compliance with these policies leads to legal actions and loss of finances, reputation, and other things. As a result, health institutions must handle patients' data in a secure way while meeting the legal requirements.

5.2.4. FINANCIAL AND RESOURCE CONSTRAINTS

Financial and technological challenges remain one of the key impediments to implementing interoperable healthcare systems and EHRs. Significant investments in terms of software, infrastructure, cloud-based solutions, cyber security measures, maintenance, and updates are crucial for implementing healthcare technology successfully. Small hospitals and care facilities find it challenging to integrate advanced interoperable systems due to inadequate financial resources for such an endeavor. The cost of ensuring that health technologies are available affects the adoption of interoperability plans and reduces the effectiveness of managing health data.

The shortage of qualified IT professionals is also a big problem in terms of making sure that goals set by the system are met. Qualified IT professionals are needed for the successful deployment of the system because they possess cybersecurity knowledge, system integration skills, and other related competencies. At the same time, many healthcare organizations face difficulties recruiting such specialists. Moreover, combining various healthcare platforms and migrating data from outdated systems into new interoperable ones is quite complicated and costly.

Training for health care professionals also takes considerable time and money. Doctors, nurses, administrators, and other healthcare technical workers need to be adequately trained on how to use electronic health record systems efficiently. Ongoing training is required since technologies used in health care are constantly developing. It means that adequate financing, governmental assistance, and smart investments will help overcome financial barriers to achieving healthcare interoperability.

5.3. PRIVACY RISKS IN CLINICAL DATA ANALYTICS

Data Privacy in Healthcare refers to the protection of sensitive patient data, which includes healthcare records, personal information and identifiers, as well as clinical data. The former type of data pertains to personal information such as name, address, contacts and identification numbers, while the latter pertains to data about a person's health, namely the diagnoses, lab reports, medication prescriptions, and clinical outcomes.

Medical data, being closely tied to patients' health conditions, is to be protected even more strictly than personal data since there are stricter ethical and regulatory standards associated with healthcare organizations and professionals. In particular, healthcare professionals and institutions are to ensure that personal data about patients is confidential, secure and consistent. To describe data about patients' health in healthcare systems, the term 'Personal Health Information (PHI)' is used.

Since today, many healthcare facilities operate electronic health records, data analysis and cloud-based healthcare services, issues concerning the protection of patient data have become especially relevant. Namely, any access to clinical data without proper authorization and the occurrence of data breaches may be damaging to patients. For this reason, it is necessary to develop adequate cybersecurity measures and implement effective regulatory requirements (Pereira, 2025).

5.3.1. UNAUTHORIZED ACCESS TO PATIENT DATA

Unlawful or unauthorized access pertains to entry into a physical or digital system without the permission of the owner or administrator of that system. Unauthorized access can be achieved through methods such as compromising on the system security protocols, breaching system vulnerabilities, or obtaining stolen login credentials for such a system. Unauthorized access is often seen as an infringement of privacy and security policies and can bring about legal, financial, or ethical repercussions.

Unlawful or unauthorized access in the healthcare cybersecurity field pertains to unlawful access to the computing systems, network resources, databases, and even EHR of healthcare organizations that contain sensitive health-related information. The access of such an incident is performed by hackers and criminals looking to illegally steal, change, or erase sensitive information contained in the health organization's network infrastructure or computing systems. But in addition to that, unauthorized access can also be achieved internally by members of the healthcare team who exceed their scope of operation while accessing sensitive patient data.

The risk of such breaches is becoming even more frightening, considering the ramifications that come with it regarding patient confidentiality, data security, and the healthcare delivery process. A breach in the confidential medical information could affect the reputation of the hospital in question as well as the entire health care delivery system, thereby exposing hospitals to sanctions. Hence, proper access control mechanisms should be developed by healthcare organizations.

5.3.2. PREVENTING UNAUTHORIZED ACCESS TO PATIENT DATA

In today's world, the vast majority of healthcare organizations employ technology to store and manage their patients' information using tools like EHRs and EMRs. Through these technologies, healthcare professionals can easily access patients' medical records, check on the progress of their treatment, and compare their results. Nevertheless, due to the nature of the information stored within healthcare institutions, ensuring its protection from any unauthorized access has become extremely important.

1. **Technical Controls for Ensuring the Security of Personal Health Information**

   It is critical to have appropriate technical controls to prevent any breach of confidentiality of personal health information. Cybersecurity controls such as antivirus, firewalls, and intrusion detection technologies can be used to safeguard electronic systems against various attacks on their networks. It is critical to ensure that software applications in the network are up-to-date and any identified vulnerabilities are fixed.

   Another way of protecting data is through encryption technology. By encrypting personal health information while in storage and transit, organizations ensure that no one who accesses the information will be able to understand what the data entails. Moreover, organizations are advised to use access control technology to limit the number of people accessing protected personal health information. This includes the use of user identification, passwords, two-factor authentication, and access permission.

2. **Employee Training and Security Awareness**

   Employee training is crucial when it comes to making sure that information belonging to patients does not fall into the wrong hands. The health care organization must hold employee training sessions in order to educate them on various aspects, including data protection policy, cyber security issues, confidentiality, and health care data management. It is important that the employees are made aware of just how important patient information is and the consequences of misusing the information.

   Health care providers also require training on various cybersecurity issues, making them familiarize themselves with the different kinds of attacks that could happen to them, such as phishing, social engineering, suspicious emails, and other security attacks. Employee training on a regular basis will ensure that they are up to date with whatever security risks exist today. Creating a culture of compliance in the health care organization ensures that security standards are adhered to.

   In conclusion, protecting patient information from any form of misuse is extremely important in guaranteeing privacy, confidentiality, and trust in the healthcare industry. This can be accomplished through employing adequate security procedures like utilizing adequate technical controls, controlling access, encryption, and adopting advanced cybersecurity tools. Meanwhile, employee education is vital in instilling in them the importance of securing sensitive information. In this case, the combination of advanced security techniques and constant training of employees is essential in guaranteeing that information is managed securely in the health industry.

5.3.3. DATA BREACHES AND CYBERSECURITY THREATS

A data breach occurs whenever there is unauthorized access, disclosure, or theft of sensitive or confidential data. The different types of data breaches include cyber hacking, insider threats, or unintentional data exposure. To sum up, a data breach means that there is a compromise of data confidentiality and security, and its impacts go beyond the compromised data.

There is an array of data that can be targeted by data breaches, which includes personal data, financial data, intellectual property, and others. There are also many purposes for which the data can be exploited, such as making money, identity theft, corporate espionage, or politically-motivated reasons. Once you understand what a data breach is all about, then you will be able to protect yourself from them.

What Are the Potential Outcomes of a Data Breach?

There are many implications associated with a data breach. Organizations stand to lose financially and may experience a damaged reputation and legal liability. An individual may be a victim of identity theft or some other form of malicious intent. There are many ramifications related to the massive amount of sensitive information that is leaked during a data breach.

For companies, data breaches may cause serious financial losses, legal repercussions, and harm their reputation. Their customers and business partners may stop trusting them, and restoring their trust may take time and money. Data breaches may usually be prevented by implementing effective cybersecurity strategies and managing risks proactively.

Socially, data breaches may cause a violation of people's privacy rights, freedom of expression, innovations, and economic development. With the rapid development of technologies, the war against data breaches will always be waged by cybersecurity experts, corporations, and governments to ensure confidentiality and trust.

What Should a Company Do After a Data Breach?

- **Conserve the Incident:** The initial phase involves conserving the incident through stopping any activity within the compromised systems, network, or account. This limits the attack and prevents any other security risks from arising while ensuring only a small area is affected.
- **Notifying the Affected:** It is imperative that businesses notify those affected by the breach in a timely manner. Information on which type of personal data was stolen needs to be included in the notification.
- **Collecting and Conserving Evidence:** Collecting and conserving evidence is important since it is used during investigations and legal actions against perpetrators. Logging all actions and keeping time stamps are helpful in such situations.
- **Conduct a Complete Investigation:** It is critical to conduct a complete investigation to understand the reason behind the breach in order to avoid any future breaches. The investigation can help in discovering the loopholes that were exploited and the measures that need to be taken in order to rectify them.
- **Improve Security Measures:** In light of the results of the investigation, firms should improve security measures to avoid future occurrences of such attacks. This could be achieved through upgrading security measures, employee training, and strengthening network security systems.

The Current Landscape of Healthcare Cybersecurity

The cybersecurity landscape facing the healthcare industry is one that is constantly changing and increasingly sophisticated and complicated. Cyberattacks on hospitals and clinics have increased drastically. As per the 2025 Verizon Data Breach Investigation Report (DBIR), in the healthcare industry alone, there were 1,710 security breaches, out of which 1,542 were data disclosures. One of the biggest security threats to healthcare today includes intrusions such as ransomware and espionage.

In recent years, phishing campaigns aimed at healthcare workers have become prevalent. As per the HHS OCR Breach Portal report, also popularly known as the "OCR Wall of Shame," in 2024, 79 healthcare providers were attacked through email due to hacking/IT incidents and unauthorized access/disclosures, affecting patient numbers from 500 to 464,159.

The data breach statistics from the 2025 statistics OCR Breach Portal are alarming as there are 39 instances of data breaches committed against healthcare organizations between January 1 to April 23. The number of patients impacted per facility is between 515 to 494,326.

The attacks can become very expensive. For example, the IBM report on the Cost of a Data Breach in 2024 showed that breaches caused by phishing averaged USD $9.77 million for each instance in the healthcare industry (Davidoff, 2019).

5.4. SECURE AI INTEGRATION IN HEALTHCARE SYSTEMS

The healthcare sector finds itself at a crossroads where AI and ML innovations have come to revolutionize patient data management by healthcare establishments. With the increasing digitization of the healthcare sector, these enterprises are encountering significant obstacles in achieving the delicate balance between ensuring access to data and meeting privacy needs, among others.

Such evolution requires highly sophisticated solutions capable of automating and optimizing the data governance methods by implementing top-notch security measures. Introduction of the "reality plus AI" approach in healthcare is quite far removed from conventional data governance solutions. Instead of cumbersome systems that may result in workflow disruptions due to their inefficiency, contemporary hospitals and other healthcare facilities opt for AI platforms that automatically recognize protected data, control its access, and adhere to such strict requirements as HIPAA, GDPR, and other regional regulations of this type.

These systems are able to comprehend the environment, recognize potential risks, and dynamically modify access controls based on real-time behavioral analysis through the use of deep learning and natural language processing technology. The role of automated policy enforcement in hospitals is crucial to the use of such technology (Imoize et al., 2023).

5.4.1. ROLE OF AI IN HEALTHCARE

According to the European Commission, AI helps in managing and distributing healthcare resources and avoiding wastage of such resources due to its ability to forecast patient admissions and the use of hospital resources. AI has the capacity to save costs.

By simplifying tasks such as scheduling, billing, and handling of electronic health records through automation and optimization, AI enables healthcare practitioners to concentrate on their work. In addition, this makes it easy to avoid over-documentation by healthcare workers, which often lead to fatigue.

AI also facilitates early diagnosis of any disease or rare diseases not easily detectable by human beings. Early diagnosis allows for early treatment, which will involve minimally invasive procedures at a relatively lower cost.

AI for Medical Diagnosis

AI technology has greatly improved the accuracy of diagnoses through the interpretation of complex medical information with great precision. With the use of machine learning and deep learning algorithms, AI can analyze large amounts of clinical information in a short time and detect hidden patterns that can enhance the ability to diagnose diseases in many different medical disciplines. Table 1 highlights the shift from conventional diagnosis to AI-assisted diagnosis.

- **AI in Radiology**

  AI-based imaging applications assist in recognizing any abnormalities within x-rays, CT scans, MRIs, and ultrasounds.

CNN is indispensable when it comes to evaluating medical images to diagnose diseases like lung nodules, brain cancers, and fractures. In addition to making radiologists' lives easier, such technologies enhance diagnostic precision by eliminating any potential human errors while improving productivity.

- **AI in Pathology**

  AI-based histopathology analysis has contributed to the advancement of digital pathology through the ability to precisely identify both malignant changes and precancerous alterations in tissues. AI can distinguish between normal and cancer cells, thus enabling physicians to deliver timely and accurate diagnostics. AI is also useful in helping physicians predict disease development and tailor treatment regimens accordingly.

- **AI in dermatology**

  Diagnostics using AI technology analyze skin disorders such as lesions, rashes, and moles that lead to various illnesses including melanoma, psoriasis, and eczema. With machine learning algorithms designed from extensive data about dermatology, it is possible to evaluate photos of the skin with almost as much precision as a dermatologist would do. Moreover, there are AI-based smartphone applications where one can photograph his/her skin and get an evaluation.

- **AI in ophthalmology**

  Through retinal imaging, AI technology has greatly aided in the detection of glaucoma, macular degeneration, and diabetic retinopathy. By identifying patterns associated with eye conditions, deep learning algorithms enable early diagnosis and treatment, preventing blindness and visual loss in high-risk individuals. In places where access to ophthalmologists is restricted, AI-assisted screening tools are particularly helpful.

- **AI in Cardiology**

  By enhancing the detection of arrhythmias, heart failure, and coronary artery disease, artificial intelligence is revolutionizing cardiology. Machine learning models examine electrocardiograms (ECGs), echocardiograms, and patient histories to detect problems that would be missed by human interpretation. AI-driven risk assessment models can also forecast an individual's risk of acquiring cardiovascular diseases based on lifestyle factors, genetic predisposition, and clinical history, allowing for preventive measures.

- **AI for Infectious Disease Detection**

  AI has aided in the diagnosis of infectious diseases such as sepsis, COVID-19, and tuberculosis. To correctly diagnose ailments, AI systems assess blood tests, chest X-rays, and patient symptoms. AI-assisted CT scan analysis has made it possible to identify virus-associated pneumonia patterns in the COVID-19 case, facilitating quicker triage and treatment.

- **AI for Multimodal Diagnosis**

  Artificial intelligence is rapidly being used for multimodal data integration, which integrates imaging, genetic, laboratory, and clinical data to improve diagnostic accuracy, in addition to single-modality diagnosis. AI-powered platforms can provide more precise and customized diagnoses by combining genetic sequencing data with radiological and pathological findings, particularly in complex diseases like cancer and neurological disorders.

To summarize, AI has revolutionized the field of healthcare through enhancing the accuracy of diagnosis, making decisions in healthcare, and improving efficiency within the healthcare sector. Various AI technologies have been adopted in fields such as radiology, pathology, cardiology, and infectious diseases for helping healthcare workers make a quicker and more accurate diagnosis. However, despite the numerous advantages of AI, issues of data privacy and security cannot be overlooked (Patil et al., 2026).

5.4.2. CHALLENGES OF AI IN HEALTHCARE

Institutions within the modern health care sector find themselves in an entirely new situation when it comes to securing their information, which is much more complex than what is encountered with any other type of information protection needs. In addition to the highly sensitive nature of the patient data, there is also the vast volume of information being collected within a variety of health care sectors and specialties, which further complicates the issue.

The very essence of the information in the field of health care poses some unique challenges that cannot be resolved using traditional methods. Patient information includes such items as basic patient data, medical history, genetic data, treatment information, and even medical imaging, each requiring special security precautions but remaining accessible at all times for health care professionals who need it for treating the patients.

Some of the main issues with traditional methods of protecting health care data include:

- **System administrator vulnerabilities:** Many conventional systems tend to provide system administrators with many privileges, posing possible dangers to security. With insufficiently segregated administration rights, a single breach into an administrative account may lead to the leakage of confidential information about patients. In order to protect patient records from any breach, hospitals require complex mechanisms to segregate access rights for administrators.
- **Manual policy enforcement:** The ever-changing landscape of healthcare, especially when patient information needs to be accessed by various departments or even from outside healthcare, renders the manual implementation of policies more difficult. Health organizations often require assistance in accessing crucial information about their patients until the manual approval process is completed.

- **Regulatory compliance complexity**: The healthcare sector is subjected to many sets of rules and regulations such as HIPAA, GDPR, and State Healthcare Privacy Rules. Keeping track of such a complex set of rules and enforcing them is highly cumbersome and increases the risk of non-compliance.

Limits of conventional methods show the dire necessity of intelligent automated systems for healthcare data management. In today's healthcare settings, solutions that can (see Figure 5.1).

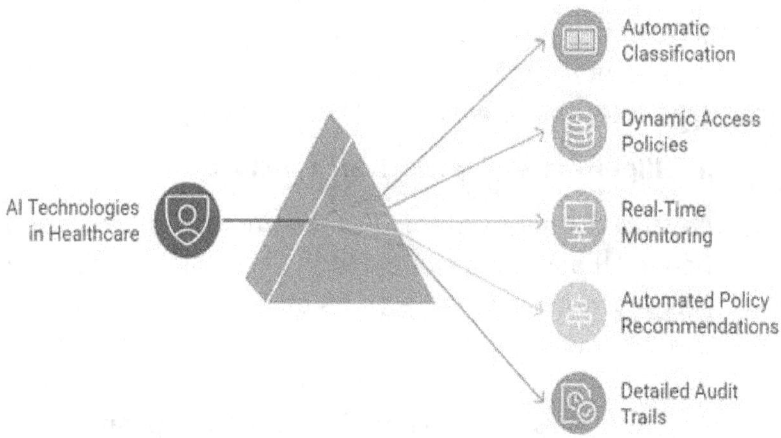

Figure 5.1: AI Technologies in Healthcare Security

The following diagram (Figure 5.1) demonstrates the role that Artificial Intelligence plays in enhancing security within healthcare IT infrastructures. The application of AI technology ensures the safety of health care data through the automation of data categorization, access control, real-time monitoring, and threat detection capabilities. In addition to that, AI assists in maintaining audit logs and regulatory compliance by logging all user actions.

To conclude, even though AI can be very beneficial for healthcare, there are certain issues that must be taken into account, such as data protection, privacy, access management, and other similar concerns. Conventional security strategies are no longer effective at addressing the complexities of healthcare data. It is imperative that the use of AI-based security solutions and data protection techniques be implemented (Panagoulias et al., 2025).

5.4.3. ADVANCED SECURITY ARCHITECTURE IN HEALTHCARE OPERATIONS

In today's environment, the current healthcare systems need security frameworks which would help in safeguarding personal health information as well as conducting safe healthcare operations. In an environment characterized by increasing adoption of technologies such as AI, EHRs, cloud systems, and other medical equipment, the need arises for adopting security frameworks that will assist in monitoring, accessing data securely, detecting risks, and protecting privacy.

1. **Intelligent safety network architecture**

   Advanced safety systems in modern healthcare settings are needed that use AI technology and act as an all-encompassing security net in all aspects of their operations. The design involves constant surveillance through sensors and analysis of data streams in real time for detecting any anomalies while ensuring privacy protection. Such systems operate in different security domains, including data access, drug dispensing, and patient care delivery, to predict any safety incidents.

   The security architecture ensures there are distinct processing routes for each safety issue, allowing an instantaneous reaction to emergency safety issues while handling the regular monitoring processes effectively. This robust framework connects with the current clinical systems using tailor-made APIs to ensure that safety monitoring is integrated into the workflow without violating HIPAA requirements. The solution uses advanced natural language processing technology to examine the communication data in clinical settings, detecting any safety issues in real-time without compromising patient data privacy.

2. **Predictive analytics and real-time monitoring systems**

   Advanced predictive analytics systems are deployed within healthcare institutions to monitor operational data for any signs of potential safety issues. The monitoring system utilizes different processing pipelines based on different security levels, allowing for optimized resource management while ensuring that sensitive data is handled appropriately. It leverages complex machine learning algorithms to predict safety issues by analyzing trends in data from different sources, such as electronic medical records, medical devices, and access logs.

   An automatic alerting system is embedded into the monitoring process to trigger notifications when there are critical safety issues, with all activities logged for auditing purposes. Machine learning models constantly learn from new trends in safety data, becoming increasingly accurate without compromising security controls. The system integrates data from multiple sources using advanced data fusion methods to generate a complete safety profile for improved risk assessment.

3. **Clinical impact implementation framework**

   Effective safety systems must incorporate measures aimed at evaluating and validating the success of the AI solutions in achieving the desired results without compromising on privacy and security. The implementation architecture sets up efficient ways to trace any improvement in safety across various aspects of the clinical environment while ensuring patient information is protected throughout the process. Advanced analytics software tools are used to gauge the impact of safety measures, thereby making decisions in terms of resource allocation and prioritizing certain strategies.

   A good AI safety system keeps track of audit trails of safety improvements and records any instance of prevention of an incident by the use of AI technology while protecting patient privacy. The system uses advanced anonymization methods to evaluate the safety improvements made without breaching

HIPAA laws. The safety system incorporates reporting capabilities aimed at analyzing the safety impact of AI solutions without violating any patient information.

This structure for measuring impact is an empirical way of showing the improvement in safety while upholding the greatest standards of privacy and data security. Healthcare organisations could demonstrate improvements in patient health without sacrificing security by regularly monitoring and analyzing safety protocols (Guo et al., 2024).

5.4.4. THE EVOLUTION OF AI-DRIVEN HEALTHCARE SECURITY

As a result of the incorporation of AI in the field of healthcare, there is a notable change regarding the ways by which the protection of patient information and health care systems is achieved. The current security practices are not enough when dealing with the ever-increasing amount of healthcare-related information that is being digitized, coupled with the associated cybersecurity threats that come with the trend. This resulted in new security practices being introduced with AI as a solution for risk management, threat detection, and better access control and privacy.

- **Advanced AI architecture evolution**

  Futuristic healthcare security systems will rely on more advanced neural network architectures. Transformer architectures will be replaced by specific architectures designed specifically for healthcare, thus integrating healthcare domain expertise into mechanisms of attentiveness. Healthcare security systems will acquire contextual awareness in both the clinical and security domains, going beyond the capabilities of existing GenAI technologies. Resistant to quantum encryption will need to be integrated into AI security systems as quantum computing becomes more advanced.

- **Autonomous security systems**

  In the future generation of data safety stands, complete automation of security operations will be accomplished through the use of reinforcement learning methods that will ensure rapid reaction to new threats. Future security systems will go beyond the present-day rule-based systems by acquiring predictive powers, allowing them to detect potential breaches before they happen. This will be possible due to the use causal AI models to support security systems determine what is behind security risks.

- **Cross-domain integration**

  The future of healthcare security systems is expected to be integrated with clinical decision support systems, leading to an interconnected system where healthcare security is intertwined with clinical practices. Real-time healthcare security decisions can be made, taking into account the requirements of data security and the needs of the patient at the moment. Using natural language processing techniques, the systems will have the ability to analyze clinical information and adapt their security measures accordingly.

- **Regulatory intelligence**

  The advancement of AI-powered security systems would incorporate the development of complex algorithms capable of understanding and enacting regulatory policies. Such systems would adapt automatically to new regulations applicable to the healthcare industry, using sophisticated language models to make changes in regulations without any human involvement. It is necessary to develop transformers specifically designed to understand regulatory language in order to achieve this goal.

- **Administrator role evolution**

  The current role of the traditional system administrator will be drastically altered with increasing automation in AI systems. The future of security will involve AI-based systems of managing the role of system administrators based on the behavioral patterns of the same and changing organizational requirements. This will result in much finer granularity and dynamism in the access control system where roles are managed and adjusted based on the learning of AI algorithms.

- **Ethical AI framework development**

  The evolution of artificial intelligence systems in healthcare would require ever-evolving ethical constructs as well. Future AI systems will possess high levels of moral reasoning, allowing them to make highly nuanced and ethically sensitive decisions about data access and security. Moreover, future AI systems will gain the ability to articulate their thought process related to making such ethical decisions.

To conclude, the advancement of AI in health care security changes the way health care organizations approach the management of their security challenges. By using cutting-edge AI solutions, health care organizations can enhance threat detection capabilities, optimize cyber operations, achieve better regulatory compliance and access control. The increasing digitization and networking of health care services makes the use of AI-powered security frameworks necessary for modern health care providers (Pratap et al., 2025).

5.5. CHAPTER SUMMARY

In this chapter, it is explained why privacy, security, and interoperability are key factors in the process of managing clinical data and developing electronic health records. The chapter defines the features and benefits of using "electronic health records" (EHRs), describing their architecture and discussing their potential application and implementation models. Furthermore, it highlights the main challenges associated with implementing EHRs in healthcare practice.

Finally, the chapter addresses some of the most common problems that arise in healthcare organizations when they try to share their data in an effective manner. Some of the major barriers to successful healthcare data sharing include technology limitations, fragmented information systems, bad quality of data, semantic differences, privacy issues, and the lack of funds and technological capabilities.

Furthermore, the chapter examined security threats related to clinical analytics such as breach of data confidentiality and integrity, cybersecurity threats, and breaches of patient information. It is imperative to ensure the application of technical controls, access control systems, data encryption tools, and training employees on how to manage PHI. The increase in cyber-attacks against health care institutions requires more proactive and effective risk mitigation and management strategies.

Finally, the chapter explored the concept of the implementation of AI technology into the healthcare sector. Various AI systems and approaches are used to support clinical decisions making, automation of business processes within the industry, cybersecurity, and protection of data from malicious actors. In addition, various challenges of the use of AI in health care sector, advanced security systems, prediction and monitoring capabilities, as well as the evolution of future security models were reviewed in the chapter. Overall, the chapter stresses the importance of developing smart and interoperable security systems in the healthcare sector.

Multiple Choice Questions (MCQs)

1. **What is the primary purpose of an Electronic Health Record (EHR)?**
   - A. To store financial data of hospitals
   - B. To digitally store and manage patient health information
   - C. To track hospital staff attendance
   - D. To manage insurance claims only
2. **Which of the following is a key component of EHR structure?**
   - A. Social media data
   - B. Patient demographics and medical history
   - C. Banking transactions
   - D. Weather data
3. **What does interoperability in healthcare refer to?**
   - A. Sharing data within a single department
   - B. Ability of systems to exchange and use data across platforms
   - C. Limiting access to patient data
   - D. Encrypting medical records
4. **Which is a major challenge in data sharing across healthcare systems?**
   - A. Excess storage capacity
   - B. Lack of standard data formats
   - C. Too many healthcare professionals
   - D. High patient satisfaction

5. **What is a common privacy risk in clinical data analytics?**
   A. Faster diagnosis
   B. Data breaches and unauthorized access
   C. Improved treatment plans
   D. Reduced costs
6. **Which technique helps protect patient privacy in data analytics?**
   A. Data duplication
   B. Data anonymization
   C. Data deletion
   D. Data compression
7. **Why is secure AI integration important in healthcare systems?**
   A. To reduce hospital staff
   B. To ensure patient data confidentiality and safety
   C. To increase advertising
   D. To replace doctors completely
8. **Which of the following is a risk of improper AI integration in healthcare?**
   A. Increased transparency
   B. Data leakage and bias
   C. Better patient outcomes
   D. Improved communication
9. **What role does encryption play in EHR systems?**
   A. It deletes unnecessary data
   B. It protects data from unauthorized access
   C. It increases data size
   D. It simplifies user interface

10. **Which regulation concept is most relevant to protecting clinical data privacy?**
    A. Open access policy
    B. Data confidentiality and compliance standards
    C. Marketing strategies
    D. Software development lifecycle

Answers

1	2	3	4	5	6	7	8	9	10
B	B	B	B	B	B	B	B	B	B

Chapter 6

APPLICATIONS OF PRIVACY-PRESERVING AI

6.1. AI IN MEDICAL IMAGING WITH PRIVACY CONSTRAINTS

The use of artificial intelligence in medical imaging can be seen as a new convergence between technology and medicine. The incorporation of artificial intelligence in medical imaging can be considered as a paradigm shift that will change the way of diagnosing and treating patients.

For instance, the application of AI and machine learning in Radiology, Nuclear Magnetic Resonance, and Medical Imaging (RNMMI) has advanced at an unprecedented pace, recording an average annual growth rate of 29.8%, with a doubling period of around 2.7 years. This is not the only medical field undergoing such an evolution; AI has the potential to facilitate the earlier detection of diseases and personalized medicine.

It has implications, particularly in areas like neurology and oncology, that require timely diagnosis. In other words, its capability to greatly improve the scanning capacity has been confirmed and it shows not only the improvement of quality and safety but also improved efficiency and cost-effectiveness. In regard to medical imaging, there are many ways how AI technologies impact it. First of all, it enhances patient treatment since the diagnosis will be more accurate and the errors will be reduced. In this respect, diseases can be diagnosed much earlier.

With the help of artificial intelligence, medical imaging becomes better in terms of diagnosing different conditions and making proper diagnoses. Yet, there should be certain techniques to ensure confidentiality of information.

6.1.1. AI-BASED IMAGE ANALYSIS AND DIAGNOSTIC APPLICATIONS

Medical imaging, whether through MRIs, pathology slides, X-rays, or CT scans, forms the basis of modern clinical diagnosis. Doctors can diagnose diseases, determine their extent, and select the most suitable treatment through these imaging techniques. But relying solely on visual inspection is becoming increasingly difficult with the growing volume and intricacy of the imaging data.

This kind of AI technology is applied in image analytics within medicine. Algorithms will detect irregularities, disease trends, and even subtle structure changes that might be difficult to spot with the naked eye using pixel-based information. For the application of artificial intelligence in medical imaging to work, visual information from pathologic slices, MRIs, CT scans, ultrasound tests, and X-rays has to be represented numerically. These pieces of information are then analyzed to classify diseases, spot irregularities, or demarcate regions of interest.

Key Applications of AI in Medical Imaging

AI is helping medicine through medical imaging through improved decision-making, image processing, and accuracy. Some applications of AI in medical imaging within radiology, pathology, cardiology, and ophthalmology are depicted in the figure below.

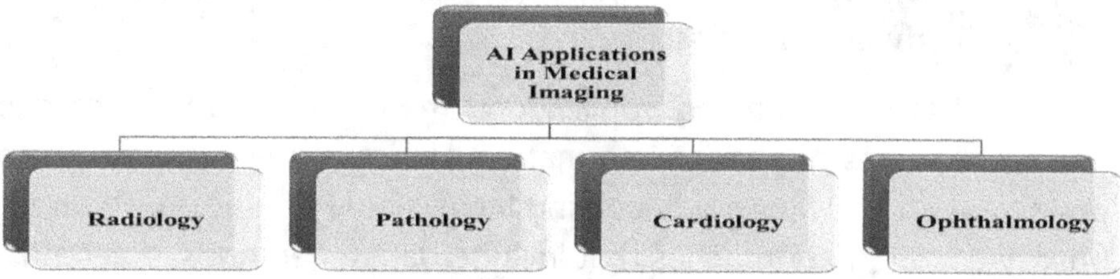

Figure 6.1: Major Applications of Medical Imaging with Artificial Intelligence

Source: Author (2026)

As shown in the below figure, it can be clearly observed that artificial intelligence technology is being implemented within medical areas like radiology, pathology, cardiology, and ophthalmology for several purposes including image processing, diagnostics, and decision making.

- **Radiology:** Artificial intelligence solutions for radiology detect diseases such as cancer, bone fractures, internal bleeding, and lung issues by examining images from X-rays, CT scans, and MRI scans. Automated triage tools assist radiologists in focusing on critical findings while prioritizing time-sensitive cases.
- **Pathology:** With the help of high-resolution slide imaging, advanced digital pathology is achieved via AI technology in pathology. The algorithms aid in detecting cancer cells, classifying different tumor types, and standardizing biopsies.
- **Cardiology**: Applications of AI technology in cardiology involve cardiac CT scans, MRI images, and echocardiography, all for the purpose of analyzing the heart's anatomy and physiology. Machine learning algorithms help classify heart disease risks, measure data points, and detect anomalies in the heart's structure.
- **Ophthalmology:** AI ophthalmology technologies examine retinal images to identify diseases like age-related macular degeneration, glaucoma, and diabetic retinopathy. Timely

intervention prior to irreparable vision loss is made possible by early, automated screening.

In AI-assisted imaging applications, there is a need for access to massive volumes of patient information. Hence, issues regarding data protection and privacy are becoming increasingly significant. There are privacy-ensuring approaches that include data federations, differential privacy, and secure encryption, among others.

Medical image analysis with artificial intelligence (AI) technology has revolutionized the field of medical diagnostics, increasing its accuracy and efficiency. Nonetheless, there is a need for privacy preservation mechanisms that will allow for the safe processing of the medical images data.

6.2.2. CHALLENGES IN AI-BASED MEDICAL DEVICES

While there has been remarkable progress made by AI in medical imaging and diagnostics, a number of technological, ethical, and legal obstacles continue to impact the widespread adoption of AI technology within healthcare environments .It is becoming more and more important to take into account numerous issues related to privacy, security, transparency, and fairness when utilizing AI in medicine because of the extremely sensitive nature of patient data and machine learning models used in diagnostic processes based on AI.

However, there are several challenges associated with the implementation of AI and image analysis in medical imaging technologies despite their many advantages. To ensure the safe and ethical implementation of these technologies, it is necessary to address these challenges.

- **Data Privacy and Security**

  Data privacy and cybersecurity are of utmost importance since medical photographs include extremely sensitive patient information. The availability of large imaging databases is essential for AI systems and poses the risk of data breach if appropriate levels of governance, encryption, and control mechanisms aren't put into place. To maintain trust with patients, compliance to health care data protection laws is essential.

Healthcare institutions have started using privacy-aware AI approaches like federated learning, differential privacy, homomorphic encryption, and SMPC (Secure Multi Party Computation) to overcome the above challenges. By adopting such methods, AI systems can be applied to study medical images without revealing any confidential information about patients.

- **Bias and Data Representativeness**

  The accuracy of the AI model itself relies heavily on the accuracy of training data. This could be biased by incomplete, imbalanced, or non-representative data sets, and could affect the accuracy of diagnostics for some categories of patients. Fairness of diagnostic outcomes is only possible with diversity among training data.

- **Regulatory and Validation Issues**

  Before being adopted as diagnostic technologies in clinical practice, the algorithms must be validated and certified through extensive procedures proving their efficacy, safety, and accuracy. The difficulty of undergoing such a lengthy and different in various regions procedure discourages the process from taking place.

- **Transparency and Explainability Problems**

  Most complex AI models, especially those based on deep learning techniques, operate as "black boxes," rendering it difficult for physicians to understand the grounds for decision-making. In cases where explainability is especially important in diagnosis, this issue becomes even more prominent.

- **Data Quality and Model Reliability**

  Performance of AI is highly contingent on the availability of quality imaging data. Diagnosis may fail miserably as a result of the presence of imaging artifact, wrong labelling, and poor image quality. Quality assurance and continuous monitoring are essential to ensure the reliable performance of an AI in practical application.

- **Considerations of Ethics and Regulations**

  Underpinning ethics, which include informed consent, data ownership, and AI system functionality should be considered for proper application of AI in medical diagnosis. Proper accountability structures play an important role in establishing the obligation of all stakeholders involved in the development and application of AI systems.

Regulation of AI applications plays a critical role in ensuring that medical AI applications are safe and reliable. The approval process before deploying medical AI technology in clinics is determined by international agencies such as FDA and CE regulatory agencies.

Although there is an array of advantages brought about by AI-based medical imaging, a number of considerations should be put into place to ensure that these systems will be effectively used in the healthcare environment. This can be achieved through the adoption of privacy-aware AI systems.

While it is true that AI-based medical imaging presents more accuracy in addition to effective healthcare delivery, there are several challenges that should be considered when trying to adopt this technology in the healthcare sector. These challenges include data security, cyber security, biases, transparency, and compliance among others.

6.1.3. PRIVACY-PRESERVING TECHNIQUES IN MEDICAL IMAGING

Privacy in AI-driven imaging in medicine has become very important because of the participation of sensitive information from patients within health care services. It is necessary to ensure that the patient's data is maintained as private and is protected throughout its life cycle in order to increase the accuracy of diagnosis. Therefore, privacy preservation technology is essential to AI powered medical imaging (Imoize et al., 2023).

Due to the cumulative usage of (AI) in medical imaging technology, the need for developing and implementing efficient privacy preservation methods has also grown. Since images obtained through procedures such as X-ray, CT, MRI, ultrasound imaging, and pathology slides can contain private patient information that can be leaked out during various stages of data processing, including data collection, storing, transmitting, and AI model training, privacy-preserving measures should be utilized to prevent any possible data breach. Thus, privacy-preserving methods have become an integral part of AI in healthcare in order to facilitate safe and ethical practices.

One of the most commonly used privacy-preserving technologies in the context of AI in healthcare is federated learning. This technique enables the collaborative training of a single AI model by different hospitals or healthcare institutions without exchanging private patient images between them, as the process takes place on a local computer of each participating institution. Moreover, the results of each round of training are transferred as encrypted model parameters that do not pose any privacy threats. The application of federated learning is highly beneficial for radiology and pathology since these two areas require access to a diverse dataset.

Differential privacy is another critical technology that is implemented to improve privacy in medical imaging systems. With the use of this privacy technology, AI systems add some controlled levels of statistical noise to both datasets and model outputs. In this way, AI makes it hard for individuals to be identified based on the data. By implementing differential privacy, healthcare professionals ensure the privacy of patients while obtaining valuable information from AI algorithms.

Homomorphic encryption is yet another important technology used to enhance privacy in medical imaging applications. In particular, with the use of this technology, it is possible to conduct calculations with the data that remains encrypted during the entire process. Thus, it becomes feasible to conduct the calculations of data from images of different patients securely. Likewise, Secure Multi-Party Calculation (SMPC) is a technique that allows several parties to calculate some values on the same dataset without disclosing their personal data.

Moreover, data anonymization and de-identification are other ways of minimizing privacy threats in medical imaging data sets. Such procedures involve eliminating personally identifiable information (PII) from medical data and imaging metadata prior to sharing or using the data in AI training. Nevertheless, anonymization might not guarantee total anonymity when dealing with large data sets. Hence, privacy-preserving AI models are frequently utilized alongside anonymization procedures.

Apart from enhancing patient privacy, privacy-preserving models enable healthcare organizations to adhere to the relevant laws that govern AI applications in the medical field. For example, the safe handling and processing of personal health information is subject to stringent regulations under HIPAA and GDPR. Consequently, including methods like encryption, differential privacy, federated learning, and secure computations allows for safe deployment of AI-driven medical imaging tools within regulatory guidelines.

In order to ensure the safe application of AI technology in medical imaging, privacy-preservation strategies are crucial. Federated learning, differential privacy, homomorphic encryption, and SMPC are just some of the techniques that could be used to ensure the confidentiality and safety of patients when using artificial intelligence for diagnostics and treatments.

6.2. PREDICTIVE ANALYTICS IN PATIENT CARE

One technique for predicting the impact of data on future health implications is through predictive analytics. Predictive analytics requires the analysis of past data to make well-informed predictions regarding what could happen next. Health records, test results, and societal issues among others make up the past data to be used for making predictions.

The prevention of disease before it happens constitutes the goal of the shift from reactive care to proactive care. Such can be made possible by modern technologies such as AI and big data.

Using advanced algorithms to make predictions about likely results makes predictive analytics improve health care processes. In essence, the process works as follows:

- **Data Integration:** A comprehensive picture of patient health is obtained by combining data from multiple sources.
- **Pattern Recognition:** AI systems look for patterns and connections in the data.
- **Forecasting:** Predictive models help predict future events such as patient readmission or how the disease will progress.
- **Decision Support:** By using insights to make proactive decisions, healthcare providers can enhance patient care and operational effectiveness.

The process of predictive modelling entails making predictions about future health care occurrences by analyzing previous data. Predictive models are created by utilizing either statistical methods or machine learning algorithms depending on the particular health care issue being addressed. The models are then tested against other sets of data to establish their validity and minimize any form of biases that may arise. Predictive models are then put into practice after validation and continuously updated with current data.

Due to the need of these systems for highly confidential personal information of patients, security and privacy issues come out to be an important part of this technology. Predictive healthcare uses privacy technology including data sharing, federated learning, and differential privacy for protecting patient's data. Due to its ability to facilitate early disease prediction and personalized medicine delivery, predictive analytics is revolutionizing the entire healthcare industry. But then again, because of extremely sensitive data involved, privacy protection measures become essential.

6.2.1. AI MODELS FOR DISEASE PREDICTION AND RISK ASSESSMENT

The application of machine learning allows for the analysis of large amounts of patient information by healthcare classification algorithms. These tools assist medical professionals in making more reliable estimates about the health risks by detecting complicated connections. Machine learning plays an important role in early and personalized diagnostics of diseases such as cancer and cardiovascular conditions. Medical diagnosis algorithms are becoming more sophisticated. Such technologies rely on information from genetic testing, medical images, and health data stored electronically. These advancements can contribute to the reduction of medical diagnostic errors and improved patients' results through aiding doctors in making better decisions. You will be able to see the influence of such technologies on healthcare later.

Key Takeaways

- Alzheimer's illness can be predicted with up to 99% accuracy by machine learning algorithms
- To determine health hazards, healthcare categorization models examine patient data.
- Disease prediction models enhance individualized care and early detection.
- To get accurate findings, medical diagnosis algorithms use a variety of data sources.
- These technologies can improve patient care and lower diagnostic mistakes.

The predictive models created to forecast diseases and risks are intended to analyze the health data and find out if there is a specific pattern relating to the disease, risk, and progression of the disease. The implementation of such predictive models will help health practitioners make informed decisions to provide treatment options to their patients. Various predictive AI models can be utilized depending on the type of health problems and health data.

In recent years, there have been many attempts to implement AI in order to predict certain diseases and evaluate risks related to patient's health. However, the utilization of AI to forecast certain diseases is fraught with considerable problems in terms of patient privacy and the protection of sensitive data.

Large-scale electronic health records, medical imaging, genomic data, and wearables—which may contain extremely sensitive information—are used by the majority of predictive healthcare systems. The majority of hospitals are using privacy-preserving AI techniques including federated learning, differential privacy, homomorphic encryption, and secure multi-party computation to address the issues that have been found.

- **Well-liked Healthcare Classification Models:** A number of classification models have become popular in healthcare predictive modelling. These models sort through patient data using machine learning algorithms. Their goal is to accurately predict illnesses or results.
- **Logistic Regression**: For applications involving binary classification, logistic regression is very useful. It is commonly used to estimate the likelihood of specific illnesses based on patient data. For instance, it assists medical professionals in assessing cancer risk by examining smoking patterns and other variables.
- **Decision Trees**: Healthcare analytics also heavily relies on decision trees. They are excellent in dividing up patient populations according to important characteristics. They are extremely useful for identifying high-risk individuals or choosing the best course of treatment because of this capability.
- **k-Nearest Neighbors (KNN):** The KNN classifier allows one to classify the patients according to how similar they are to other patients. The algorithm performs quite well in diagnosing very rare illnesses since one of the major challenges is data scarcity.

- **Hybrid Models:** Hybrid algorithms that combine elements of clustering and classification and also classifiers in general are being increasingly used. Such methods tend to perform very well in classifying healthcare data

Model	Strengths	Healthcare Applications
Logistic Regression	Simple, interpretable	Disease risk assessment
Decision Trees	Visual, easy to understand	Treatment pathway decisions
KNN	Effective with limited data	Rare disease diagnosis
Hybrid Models	Improved performance	Complex disease prediction

The following table highlights several of the most frequently used AI-based classification models in healthcare analytics, including their benefits and uses. Such AI-based models for classification may also be applied in order to forecast the emergence of diseases, perform risks assessments, develop treatment plans, and assist in diagnosing diseases.

The use of the technology of AI to build disease forecasting and risk assessment systems has led to a revolution in the modern health sector by means of early diagnosis, personalized treatments, and decisions based on data analysis. Indeed, the potential power of machine learning may be utilized in analyzing healthcare data in order to discover certain trends and forecast the future emergence of certain diseases. However, there is no doubt that with such sensitive data, major security problems arise.

6.2.2. PRIVACY CHALLENGES IN PATIENT DATA ANALYTICS

There is a digital tsunami that has hit the healthcare industry, especially in the era of COVID-19. Digital technology, like wearable devices and gadgets, telemedicine consultations, and sophisticated predictive analytics, is everywhere trying to meet customers' demands for personalized care.

With telemedicine and electronic health records being widely used nowadays, worries over privacy of patients' personal information have risen. It is patients' right to have access to their health records either stored electronically or physically, and it is necessary for physicians and other healthcare institutions to act upon these rights.

The application of AI algorithms for predicting the state of affairs in the sphere of health care has caused concerns regarding proper data protection and patients' privacy. Predictive medicine requires access to large amounts of data available from such sources as electronic medical records, wearable devices, genomics databases, and remote monitoring systems. The data utilized by AI algorithms in the process of predictive modeling may involve sensitive personal data and pose a threat to data leaks, breaches, and misuses when data is analyzed within an AI algorithm training and distribution procedure.

A national law called the HIPAA Privacy Rule safeguards PHI, limiting its accessibility to certain entities. Any type of protected health information, whether it be verbal, written, or electronic, is subject to the Privacy Rule. Only authorized individuals should be permitted to access, store, and transmit patient data, according to these two HIPAA regulations.

Common security and privacy concerns in healthcare

Hospitals must handle the security risks associated with today's internet technology tools and platforms in order to maintain HIPAA compliance. Among these security obstacles are:

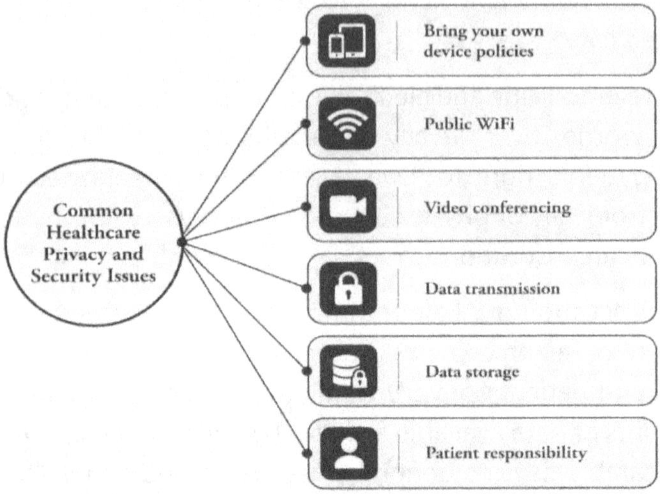

Figure shows the core problems associated with the privacy and security of healthcare information regarding access, transfer, storage, and digital communication. It highlights the importance of implementing robust cybersecurity and privacy-oriented healthcare solutions.

- **Bring your own policies for your devices**

  Bring-your-own-device (BYOD) rules are becoming more common in the healthcare sector since staff productivity, efficiency, and workflow are improved by their familiarity with using personal devices in hospitals. However, one of the biggest healthcare IT difficulties for hospital administrations is the lack of control over the usage of personal mobile devices, which may include sensitive patient PHI.

- **Public WiFi**

  Wi Fi is a highly valued convenience in coffee shops, airports, and other public gathering areas. However, regardless of the technology employed, healthcare facilities are required to take safety measures to protect PHI because they are HIPAA-covered entities. This includes taking precautions like encrypting all data, sending PHI over unprotected networks, and avoiding connecting mobile devices used to access PHI to public Wi Fi.

- **Video conferencing**

  Because video conferencing platforms like Skype and Zoom are not always HIPAA-compliant, it becomes crucial to consider things like the video's background and who else can hear what is being discussed in the office.

- **Data transmission**

  It becomes important to take into account things like the background of the video and whether else may hear what is being spoken in the office because video conferencing systems like Skype and Zoom are not always HIPAA-compliant.

- **Data storage**

  Ransomware attacks targeting healthcare institutions have brought about an urgent need for the implementation of effective data storage solutions. The attacks target healthcare information and affect the smooth running of hospitals by blocking access to critical healthcare data. For security reasons, hospitals should embrace data security measures that include limited access to healthcare data, use of encryption, two-factor authentication, monitoring of data security systems, conducting penetration tests, and educating employees about cybersecurity.

- **Patient accountability**

  Patients are not subject to HIPAA regulations; only hospitals and health institutions are. However, this does not absolve them of the need to safeguard their PHI.

  Patients must also take security precautions in order to access PHI electronically. Encrypting in-home Wi Fi routers, changing passwords periodically, and cautioning patients not to read unexpected emails—especially those with attachments that can contain malware—are all smart ideas. That's an excellent concept for any sensitive data, not just their health information.

6.2.3. FEDERATED LEARNING FOR PREDICTIVE HEALTHCARE SYSTEMS

Federated learning is a promising privacy-preserving method for predictive healthcare. The sensitive information about patients' medical conditions often needs to be obtained and stored by AI-based health care systems from multiple sources such as clinics, hospitals, wearable technology, and electronic health records. For this reason, implementation of this type of data management can pose a risk of breaches, illicit use, and privacy violation. In turn, the federated learning approach allows for training AI algorithms on medical data without having to share this data by hospitals and other health care organizations.

The ability to enhance accuracy of the AI algorithms through use of a variety of data sets from different companies is the second advantage worth mentioning in relation to the concept of federated learning in predicting healthcare outcomes. The process of training algorithms using the small number of data may result in biased and incorrect predictions. The key importance of federated learning is that the collaboration in improving the accuracy of predictive analysis can take place between healthcare institutions without sharing their private data sets (Hassan et al., 2023).

Other types of privacy protection exist on FL platforms which can be used together with those previously discussed. Such techniques include secure aggregation, differential privacy, and encryption. This allows healthcare companies to use predictive analytics and comply with all relevant legislation related to data privacy.

An AI technique called federated learning protects patient data privacy y while training machine learning algorithms. (Anandan et al., 2026). Through federated learning, medical institutions can build machine learning models through collaboration without exchanging sensitive patient information.

Applications of Federated Learning in Healthcare

- **Pharmaceutical Industry Applications**

  When it comes to pharmaceuticals, federated learning helps different institutions train AI models in drug discovery without compromising any proprietary information.

- **Personalized Medicine and Genomics**

  Personalized medicine can be achieved through federated learning because it allows the analysis of patient-specific data along with genomic information from several healthcare facilities. The use of these algorithms for AI allows predicting patient treatment responses based on their genetic variants without sharing their genetic details.

- **Generative AI for Healthcare**

  Federated learning technology is used to develop generative artificial intelligence systems for health care, including medical language models and AI assistants. Federated learning technology is used to develop generative artificial intelligence systems for health care, including medical language models and AI assistants. Hospitals may utilize local clinical notes and patient communications to train AI models without leaking confidential healthcare information.

Federated learning has become increasingly significant in recent years as a privacy-preserving technique that facilitates cooperation through keeping patient data from different healthcare institutions confidential while utilizing artificial intelligence to provide health care services.

Federated learning can help maintain privacy when developing predictive models in health care because it facilitates the ability to train machine learning models remotely without downloading sensitive data. Therefore, federated learning facilitates the use of data from different health facilities in order to improve prediction while maintaining the confidentiality of sensitive patient data.

6.3. DRUG DISCOVERY AND CLINICAL TRIALS

For the assurance that a newly developed treatment is safe and effective, a number of complex processes are undertaken during the process of drug development and research. It typically takes 12-15 years for the development of a new drug from the time of drug discovery to its market entry. When there is no effective treatment for a certain illness or the current medicines are insufficiently potent, the drug discovery process starts with an unmet medical need. Analysing biological systems and figuring out how changing a particular protein or pathway might have a therapeutic effect is the first step. Before moving on to the next phase, more validation could be necessary if an appropriate target has been found. AI and machine learning technologies have uses in drug discovery, such as speeding up chemical screening, predicting molecular interactions, and identifying possible therapeutic compounds. Large biological data sets are being combined with deep learning approaches to improve lead optimization and hit detection (Ng, 2015).

However, one drawback of using AI technology to find novel medications is that it requires access to private data from clinical trials, genetics, and biology. Pharmaceutical companies and organizations may train AI without disclosing confidential patient information and data thanks to AI technologies like federated learning, homomorphic encryption, and secure multiparty computations.

Small-molecule compounds or biological therapies are tested during the drug discovery process to find first candidates acting on the target, or hits. These hits are developed into leads with enhanced drug-like qualities. Lead optimization in drug development reveals possible drug candidates by improving the potency, selectivity, and pharmacokinetic profile of promising leads to make sure they satisfy therapeutic needs.

The Five Steps of the Drug Discovery Process

1. **Initial Drug Discovery**

   Strategic study to identify proteins, genes, or pathways as therapeutic targets is the first step in early drug discovery.

Additional target validation guarantees the therapeutic impact of acting on the chosen biomolecule.

High-content, high-throughput, or virtual screening are then used to screen thousands of molecules. These well-liked drug discovery screening methods help identify hits that interact with the target. In order to identify leads, these hits move through the hit-to-lead phase, which refines potential candidates according to biological activity, potency, and selectivity.

2. **The clinical stage**

   Human clinical trials are part of the clinical phase of the drug development process. This comprises manufacturing data, clinical protocols suggested for the clinical trials, and animal efficacy and toxicity data collected during pre-clinical investigations.

   The clinical trial begins and the potential medications move on to the next stages if it is approved:

   - **Phase I:** To assess safety and pharmacokinetics, dose, absorption, metabolism, and elimination, as well as potential side effects, the medication is administered to a small group of healthy volunteers (20–100).
   - **Phase II:** In phase II clinical trials, the drug is tested on 100 to 500 individuals having the targeted condition to assess the effectiveness of the medicine, its dose, and side effects, if any. Phase IIa studies concentrate on determining the dose of the medicine needed for effective treatment, whereas Phase IIb determines the efficacy of the medicine.
   - **Phase III:** Large-scale clinical trials of 300–3,000 participants verify the medication's efficacy and track uncommon and long-term side effects in a variety of patient demographics.

3. **Regulatory Approval**

   A New Drug Application (NDA) is submitted to regulatory bodies after a successful phase III clinical trial. To make sure the medication satisfies safety and efficacy requirements, this step entails a thorough examination of clinical data, manufacturing procedures, and labelling. The "risk-benefit ratio" of the medication must be favorable. If successful, these reviews—which often take one to two years—lead to regulatory approval.

4. **Clinical Trials**

   Human subjects are used in clinical trials to evaluate the safety, effectiveness, dosage, and side effects of newly created medications. Phases I, II, and III of clinical trials are often distinguished by a progressive rise in the number of participants. AI improves clinical trial monitoring, disease prediction, and recruiting. However, private AI systems, such as differential privacy and federated learning, safeguard confidential patient information. (Chow & Liu, 2004).

5. **Post-Market Surveillance**

   Following a drug's approval for market release, post-market surveillance takes place. During this stage, the medication's effectiveness and safety as well as any unusual adverse effects are closely monitored. In this stage, monitoring real-world health care data and patient reports using AI technology is essential, and privacy-preserving AI is key.

By employing privacy-preserving methods in the creation of AI applications, the following solutions have been discovered to address the issues raised above. First, by training models with data from several organizations without utilizing unprocessed patient data, federated learning enables collaborative model development. Second, model output cannot expose any specific patient information due to differential privacy.

Drug discovery and development is a lengthy and intricate journey, which makes sure that new medicines are not just safe but effective as well. The journey starts from identifying potential targets and goes through various stages including preclinical studies and multiple phases of clinical trials until approval by regulatory authorities.

6.3.1. AI APPLICATIONS IN DRUG DISCOVERY

Many people see the process of finding and developing new drugs as being incredibly uncertain, expensive, and time-consuming. A new drug's journey from concept to market has historically taken ten to fifteen years, with prices frequently surpassing $2 billion due to significant failure rates at every step.

However, the pharmaceutical sector is undergoing a revolutionary change due to the quick development of AI. In addition to simplifying current procedures, AI is facilitating the identification of novel medicines, improving clinical trials, and customizing therapy regimens. This study will examine how AI is affecting drug development at different phases, the difficulties it encounters, and the technology's promise in the future (Li & Corey, 2013).

Introduction to Artificial Intelligence in Drug Discovery

Artificial Intelligence is a concept that may be described as the capacity of computer systems to learn, analyze, decide, and even understand human speech. In case of drug discovery, artificial intelligence refers to machine learning algorithms capable of processing large data volumes pertaining to biology, chemistry, and clinical medicine.

There are several key areas where AI has advanced significantly in drug discovery:

- **Data Mining and Integration:** The technology of AI can help process complicated data from different sources in biology and chemistry, such as genomics and proteomics. After discovering certain patterns within this information, AI systems can provide possible drug targets or even drug candidates.
- **Predictive Modelling:** Predictive modelling through artificial intelligence techniques negates the need for costly and time-intensive tests within laboratories to identify the biological activity of new molecules/chemicals. Discovery efficiencies can be significantly enhanced, for example, through deep learning

algorithms that predict the interaction between a drug and its targeted protein molecule.

- **Laboratory Operations Automation:** Artificial intelligence-assisted laboratory operations automation technologies could help in speeding up the development of chemical compounds, high throughput screening, and many other steps involved in drug discovery processes.

Drug Identification and Validation of the Target

One of the most important and difficult stages in the drug development process is identifying and validating therapeutic targets. Traditional methods often involve manually searching for potential targets by analyzing gene expression data or protein interactions. However, these methods are labour- intensive and can lead to inaccurate or incomplete results.

AI has revolutionized this phase by enabling target identification through the integration of various omics data (genomic, transcriptomic, proteomic, etc.). By analyzing large datasets, AI algorithms can identify potential biomarkers or proteins that play key roles in diseases for instance, AI has been effectively utilized to find cancer targets that were previously missed, allowing for the creation of innovative targeted treatments.

Drug Discovery: Hit Identification and Lead Optimization

Once the targets for drugs have been recognized, then comes the stage of hit discovery, whereby those compounds that are active on the targets are chosen. Conventional HTS is very expensive and time-consuming because it tests many compounds. AI facilitates the process by employing virtual screening techniques, whereby machine learning algorithms determine the likelihood of interaction between the compounds and the target, thus prioritizing them. Additionally, AI assists in the PK/PD optimization process, whereby absorption, distribution, metabolism, excretion, and toxicity are predicted beforehand.

Preclinical and Clinical Trial Optimization

The preclinical phase, which entails assessing the effectiveness and safety of the drug on animals, is yet another area that has demonstrated significant promise for the use of artificial intelligence. Using information from past studies on animals, AI can help to determine how successful a particular drug may be when tested in a clinical study. This in turn will assist in decreasing the number of failures during human clinical trials.

Clinical trials now utilize the technology of AI to solve issues relating to data analysis, monitoring of data, and patient recruitment. Patient recruitment, for example, is among the most challenging and laborious processes in conducting clinical trials. EHRs can be analysed using AI algorithms that will identify those patients who meet specific eligibility criteria.

AI in Biomarker Discovery and Personalized Medicine

Personalized medicine is defined as a drug development method that has become more popular, especially in oncology because there are many genes that affect treatment reactions. AI is a powerful tool for discovering new biomarkers which refer to molecules that may predict disease outcomes or medication efficacy.

Using AI can help identify the genetic changes or gene expression profiles that correspond to disease outcomes and medication susceptibility using genomic data in large datasets. Such information can then help develop drugs based on the genetic information of some people. The use of AI will also prevent unnecessary treatments while reducing side effects by knowing those people who can benefit from a certain medication.

Through target identification, chemical screening, lead optimization, and clinical trials, artificial intelligence has accelerated drug discovery and development. The machine-learning models are applied in analysing large biological and clinical data to make predictions about drug action and targets. They also facilitate personalizing medicine, enhance recruitment, discover biomarkers, and increase trial effectiveness in the process of drug development.

6.3.2. SECURE COLLABORATIVE AI IN PHARMACEUTICAL RESEARCH

Increasingly, drug development requires a close relationship among hospitals, research organizations, and pharmaceutical companies. However, because patient data, including genetic information, electronic health records, and information about therapeutic trials, can be private, this cooperation is typically limited by privacy regulations. A solution to this problem comes through secure collaborative AI, which implies that several stakeholders collaborate on training and utilizing AI models, but do not share their data directly.

Federated learning is one of the most commonly used methods of secure collaborative AI. Under federated learning, each organization trains its own AI models locally, but the updates to these models are transferred to the cloud-based server. This approach ensures both collective intelligence and patient data security. Another popular method is differential privacy, where artificial noise is added to patients' data or AI models.

Differential privacy (DP) adds mathematical noise to the model updating or output to further enhance privacy promises. This prevents any individual's medical record from being inferred, even when the model parameters themselves are disclosed. This becomes especially important during clinical trials, where the risks of patient data re-identification may be substantial.

Further cryptography techniques might also be useful for ensuring effective collaboration between participants. Through the implementation of SMPC technologies, it is feasible to conduct calculations of any analytical function using private data without disclosing the data to other participants. In addition, HE technologies enable the performance of such operations on encrypted data leading to the formation of encrypted results that may be decrypted by authorized personnel only. Despite the complexity of calculations involved, such technologies can be of great value when dealing with critical tasks within pharmaceutical businesses.

These techniques assist in pharmaceutical procedures that involve cooperative target identification for drugs, biomarker identification privately, analysis of clinical trials distributive, and modelling patient enrolment for hospitals. As an instance, several hospitals can collaboratively build an AI model predicting patients' reactions to oncology medicines without exchanging data about their health status. This approach is effective both legally and scientifically.

In summary, secure collaborative AI presents an effective tool that strikes a balance between innovation and privacy, making large-scale drug research possible without violating current data protection policies.

6.4. REMOTE MONITORING AND WEARABLE DEVICES

One of the key use cases for privacy-enhancing AI technology is remote monitoring and wearables in the context of health care. Patients' vital signs, such as heart rate, blood pressure, oxygenation, sleep, and physical activity, are continuously recorded by these wearable devices. They can be utilized for early disease identification, chronic illness management, and remote patient monitoring.

AI systems will be able to analyze ongoing health data, identify any anomalies, track the course of diseases, and assist in creating customized treatment regimens. Nevertheless, the use of wearable devices produces very sensitive personal information, which poses serious issues concerning privacy, security of data, and any form of breach of data. Privacy-preserving AI approaches like federated learning make it possible to train the model using data from the user's device without any exchange of data. Differential privacy ensures that the data cannot be used to identify an individual. Wearable devices and privacy-preserving AI technologies combine to provide a smart way of conducting health care monitoring (Eappen et al., 2025).

6.4.1. AI-DRIVEN REMOTE PATIENT MONITORING AND DATA PRIVACY

Privacy-preserving AI has been used in the development of remote patient monitoring (RPM) systems which have become very useful in modern healthcare. RPM systems incorporate wearable devices, biosensors, smartwatches, and mobile apps that continually collect physiological information about patients in form of heartbeat, blood pressure, oxygen saturation, glucose level, sleep behavior, and exercise. Remote patient monitoring allows for personalized care through continued monitoring of individuals even when away from clinical settings.

Artificial intelligence becomes essential in data analysis, especially when a large amount of data is collected in real-time. Machine learning technologies can detect unusual physiological information in the body of the individual and can predict disease progression in the future. Heart disease, diabetes, respiratory conditions, and post-operative complications are just a few of the disorders that this technology may alert people to.

However, remote monitoring technologies have some disadvantages that need to be considered when implementing them. The primary problem associated with these technologies is related to their ability to collect sensitive personal health information constantly. The unauthorized access to information, weak encryption used for wireless communications, vulnerability of cloud servers, and data exchange among medical organizations are potential threats to privacy and cybersecurity.

The implementation of privacy-preserving artificial intelligence can mitigate some of the mentioned threats in particular, federated learning is utilized to train AI models on hospital servers or wearable technology without transferring unprocessed patient data to central servers. Additionally, in order to thwart any attempts to identify a particular patient, differential privacy algorithms introduce noise into the model's output. Edge AI is another promising technology for processing wearable data since the use of edge AI will decrease the use of cloud services.

Other methods that may be considered for keeping information confidential include encrypted information transmission and the usage of distributed data exchange systems. This way, an AI-powered remote monitoring system will allow obtaining correct and constant insights in the area of healthcare while maintaining confidentiality. AI-powered remote patient monitoring coupled with privacy-preserving methods facilitates a safe and intelligent patient- centered healthcare system.

6.4.2. PRIVACY RISKS IN WEARABLE HEALTHCARE DEVICES

Smartwatches, fitness bands, biosensors, and wearable ECG monitors are examples of wearable health tracking devices that continuously produce enormous amounts of personal health data, including blood glucose levels, heart rate, sleep patterns, physical activity data, and location data. Although these wearable gadgets significantly aid in the advancement of effective patient care, they also pose significant risks to patient privacy and the security of medical data.

Insecure data collection and sharing through Internet and cloud services is one big threat to patients' health data. Personal health data collected through wearable devices is vulnerable when these devices use insecure Internet connections for data transmission. Moreover, wearable devices collect behavioural patterns of patients that might assist hackers in recognizing patients when data sets are anonymous.

Another crucial concern is the accessibility of data by third parties who can potentially access wearable health data through many of the applications used to analyze them. These applications often exchange health data with health care professionals or insurance companies, raising privacy issues about misappropriation of well-being statistics, profiling, and patients' inability to protect their private data.

The use of artificial intelligence to wearable healthiness care technology can create other concerns about privacy associated with large amounts of data being aggregated and used to train AI models. Such models will have to be trained using large volumes of data, which might include confidential health data.

To address these problems, privacy-focused AI algorithms like federated learning, differential privacy, secure encryption, and edge AI are being used in wearable health care devices. These algorithms ensure the security of the data while minimizing the need to exchange the raw data in a centralized manner. In summary, protecting the privacy risks associated with wearable health care devices is necessary for developing a reliable AI health care system that can monitor health while protecting user privacy.

6.5. CHAPTER SUMMARY

The current chapter provided an overview of the uses of privacy-preserving artificial intelligence in healthcare and analyzed the changes that have been made by advanced AI technologies in the current medical field. The discussion covered the use of AI technology in imaging, predictive analytics, disease prediction, drug discovery, clinical trial design, remote monitoring, and wearable healthcare devices. Using AI in the medical field enhances diagnostic capabilities, personalizes treatments, detects diseases early, and improves clinical decision-making based on healthcare data analysis.

In addition, the chapter addressed some of the privacy and security issues that may arise from using AI technology in the healthcare sector. These may be related to risks such as data breaches, access control, patient re-identification, data transfer insecurity, and adherence to regulations. Given that there is reliance on electronic health records, medical imaging data, genomics, and wearable devices' data, patient privacy in AI healthcare technologies is essential.

The chapter discussed various AI-based strategies, including federated learning, differential privacy, homomorphic encryption, secure multi-party computation, data anonymization, and edge AI, to address the aforementioned problems. By employing their aggregate healthcare data, these methods assist hospitals, pharmaceutical companies, and research labs in training AI algorithms without directly exchanging patient data. Moreover, the chapter pointed out the significance of ethical factors, transparency, equity, cybersecurity, and healthcare regulations like HIPAA and GDPR.

Further, the chapter noted that privacy-preserving AI can be applied in drug discovery and clinical trials to enhance the process of identifying targets, screening compounds, recruiting patients, and analysing predictive insights with biomedical data and clinical trial data while preserving privacy. In addition, the chapter talked about wearable technology and remote monitoring tools and their privacy implications due to continuous health data gathering.

Hence, it was evident from the above chapter that privacy-preserving AI has become essential for developing reliable and intelligent healthcare systems. By using different privacy technologies along with AI-powered healthcare applications, healthcare professionals can achieve innovation in the sector as well as improved results for their patients.

Multiple Choice Questions (MCQs)

1. **What is the main goal of privacy-preserving AI in medical imaging?**
   A. To increase image resolution
   B. To protect patient data while enabling analysis
   C. To replace radiologists completely
   D. To reduce storage requirements
2. **Which technique is commonly used to ensure privacy in AI-based medical imaging?**
   A. Data compression
   B. Encryption and anonymization
   C. Image cropping
   D. Manual labeling
3. **Predictive analytics in patient care primarily helps in:**
   A. Designing hospital buildings
   B. Forecasting patient outcomes and risks
   C. Printing medical reports
   D. Managing hospital finances
4. **Which of the following is a benefit of predictive analytics in healthcare?**
   A. Increased paperwork
   B. Delayed diagnosis
   C. Early disease detection
   D. Reduced data usage

5. **In drug discovery, privacy-preserving AI helps by:**
   A. Sharing all patient data publicly
   B. Eliminating the need for trials
   C. Enabling secure data collaboration
   D. Reducing chemical reactions
6. **Clinical trials benefit from privacy-preserving AI by:**
   A. Ignoring patient consent
   B. Protecting sensitive participant data
   C. Removing trial phases
   D. Increasing trial costs
7. **What role do wearable devices play in healthcare AI?**
   A. Only for entertainment
   B. Monitoring patient health in real time
   C. Replacing doctors entirely
   D. Storing hospital records
8. **Remote monitoring systems are useful because they:**
   A. Require patients to stay in hospitals
   B. Provide continuous health data remotely
   C. Eliminate the need for devices
   D. Increase manual work
9. **Which privacy risk is associated with wearable devices?**
   A. Battery drain
   B. Data leakage of personal health information
   C. Screen damage
   D. Connectivity issues

10. **A key challenge in privacy-preserving AI across healthcare applications is:**
    A. Lack of electricity
    B. Balancing data utility and privacy
    C. Too many doctors
    D. Excess storage space

Answers

1	2	3	4	5	6	7	8	9	10
B	B	B	C	C	B	B	B	B	B

Chapter 7

FUTURE TRENDS AND ETHICAL CONSIDERATIONS

7.1. EMERGING TECHNOLOGIES IN PRIVACY-PRESERVING AI

Innovative technologies that have not yet reached their full potential in terms of development or practical applications are known as emerging technologies. These technologies are mostly brand-new, but they also include some under development or anticipated to be accessible within the next five to ten years. These technologies frequently signify important improvements or upgrades to current systems.

By eliminating inefficiencies, automating processes, and reducing human error, the application of emerging technology offers ground-breaking prospects to support company growth. Businesses may devote more time to other areas, especially in the financial sector, by using AI to help with repetitive tasks like data analysis, fraud detection, and compliance.

Even if the applications and advantages of emerging technologies can be alluring, their integration is still difficult and costly, requiring committed teams and participation from a variety of stakeholders. While big organisations can spend a lot of money on AI-powered solutions, smaller companies might not be able to afford such expenditures (Lilhore et al., 2024).

7.1.1. HOMOMORPHIC ENCRYPTION AND SECURE COMPUTATION TECHNIQUES

A complex type of cryptography known as "homomorphic encryption" (HE) enables direct computation on encrypted material without the need for decryption.

HE and secure computation are two key privacy technologies that allow for safe processing of confidential health data without revealing the patient's personal details. The technology allows for the development of AI-powered health care apps, secure cloud computing, and safe health data exchange.

Fundamentally, HE permits computation on encrypted data. Only the appropriate person with the decryption key will be able to view the results, which will remain encrypted. Therefore, information remains secure in processing information in a potentially untrusted environment.

Homomorphic encryption helps in making use of artificial intelligence technologies to perform analysis of information such as EHR, medical images, genome databases, and more without revealing any information related to the patient. Through this approach, hospitals can safely carry out analysis as well as collaboration without breaching any law.

- HE provides a solution to the "data in use" security problem. In general, there were ways to protect the data when it was "at rest" or "in transit." However, when it comes to data being used for computations, it must be decrypted, which opens the data to potential threats.
- HE solves this issue by enabling computation of the data without actually decrypting it. Thus, the confidentiality of the data is maintained at all stages of its lifecycle. For instance, computations can take place within a cloud environment without the customer's data being disclosed.
- During encryption, HE maintains the data's structure. Data is first encoded in a mathematical entity and then encrypted without affecting the information it contains. This makes it

possible to perform calculations on encrypted data without having to decrypt it.

- HE opens up new avenues for cooperation and safe data processing. It allows businesses to use third-party services without jeopardizing the protection of their data.
- HE makes outsourced computing and safe cloud services possible. Businesses can use cloud resources for sophisticated data analysis without disclosing private information to the cloud provider. This ability is especially useful in intelligent health care systems that use cloud computing technologies for predicting diseases, analysing medical images, practicing personalized medicine, and protecting patients' confidentiality.
- HE broadens the definition of encryption to include "data in use" (data being processed, viewed, updated) in addition to "data at rest" and "data in transit."
- HE removes the requirement to decrypt data prior to calculation. When using third-party services, this lessens or even removes privacy problems.

Selecting the best strategy for particular use cases, which are covered in the next section, requires an understanding of the various HE scheme types.

HE is one of the most crucial privacy-preserving AI techniques due to its ability to enable machine learning algorithms to perform analysis on encrypted health records without accessing sensitive personal information.

The use of homomorphic encryption permits actions to be carried out on encrypted medical data without compromising confidentiality. This technique ensures secure AI analysis, encrypted machine learning, and privacy-based cooperation between healthcare providers, thus constituting a vital technology for a secure and intelligent healthcare system.

7.1.2. SYNTHETIC DATA GENERATION AND PRIVACY-ENHANCED DATA SHARING

The use of synthetic data creation and privacy-preserving data exchange represents the latest innovations in ensuring the development of AI systems by healthcare enterprises without compromising the security of patient data. The creation of synthetic data from medical datasets will allow for AI training without exposing any confidential patient data.

Healthcare organisations are attempting to use both structured and unstructured synthetic data to address their most urgent real-world data challenges as a result of new developments and applications in machine learning models and artificial intelligence, such as generative AI, generative adversarial networks, computer vision, and transformers. Unstructured synthetic data types are qualitative and include text, photos, and video, whereas structured synthetic data types are quantitative and include tabular data, such as numbers or values.

Synthetic data is data that is artificially created but mimics actual data in all ways except for containing identifiable information. It is becoming more and more common to use synthetic data in many different industries for the purpose of advancing the fields of artificial intelligence, privacy, and business innovation.

They have already identified and investigated a number of practical applications for synthetic data, including:

- Creating fake tabular data to boost edge cases and sample size. To enhance AI model training and prediction accuracy, you can integrate this data with actual datasets.
- Producing artificial test data to speed up the testing, refinement, and verification of new features and applications.
- Using artificial data created from agent-based simulations to investigate "what-if" situations or novel business occurrences.

Synthetic data increases AI model accuracy, accelerates testing and validation processes, allows scenario analysis, protects sensitive information, and facilitates safe data exchange and collaboration.

Synthetic data can still reveal "personally identifiable information" (PII) when used as training data for AI models, despite being regarded as artificial data or "fake data" because it is computer-generated rather than produced by real events (such as electronic health records, medical imaging, genomic datasets, and clinical reports). For example, if a corporation prioritizes accuracy when creating synthetic data, the output may unintentionally contain an excessive number of personally identifiable characteristics, raising the company's vulnerability to privacy risks.

Secure deployment environments (on-premises, private cloud, or hybrid systems) should be used by organizations managing sensitive patient information for creating synthetic data sets using sensitive patient data.

Methods for Ensuring Privacy and Criteria for Assessing Synthetic Data

Data synthesis has become one of the methods for safeguarding privacy in the health sector, whereby data can be created synthetically to simulate real patient data with minimum risks of privacy breaches. It is useful in training AI models and also in conducting research.

Data Synthesis for Secure Healthcare Usage

Data synthesis helps healthcare institutions develop artificial data that maintains the properties of original patient data without revealing sensitive data entries. The artificial data is helpful in conducting research and developing AI models among others.

Privacy Safeguard and Strong Control Methods

Healthcare institutions that use synthetic data must employ techniques for protecting privacy while creating data. Differential privacy is a commonly employed mechanism that involves adding random noise to the data, thus making it impossible to identify individuals in the dataset.

Metrics for Assessing Privacy in Synthetic Data

In cases where differential privacy is not employed, organizations must measure privacy exposure through appropriate metrics to guarantee secure data sharing and privacy levels.

- **Leakage Score:** Indicates the extent to which data records overlap between the original and synthetic datasets. Leakage score is high when there is a large overlap, which results in privacy vulnerability and potential exposure of confidential data.
- **Proximity Score:** Assesses the gap between original and synthetic data. A small distance implies greater proximity and re-identification likelihood, whereas a large distance enhances privacy.

The use of synthetic data in the domain of healthcare can guarantee the use of secure applications as this data provides patient data that is not private in nature. There are privacy techniques such as differential privacy and privacy measures such as leakage score and proximity score that ensure privacy.

Synthetic data and privacy-preserving sharing aid in healthcare AI in terms of training and testing and sharing the data without actually utilizing patient data. Nevertheless, it poses an issue of data leakage unless taken into consideration, hence the need for methods such as differential privacy.

7.1.3. QUANTUM-SAFE CRYPTOGRAPHY AND NEXT-GENERATION PRIVACY SOLUTIONS

These codes, keys, encryption systems, and authentication schemes are just mathematical puzzles meant to be challenging for traditional computers to solve. Because all those mathematical problems are difficult for traditional computers to solve yet their solutions are simple to verify, public-key algorithms perform well.

RSA is based on prime factorization, which is easy for quantum computers but hard for classical computers. Even then, the most powerful classical supercomputers would still not be able to Read the encoded message by breaking down the 2048-bit integer into its constituent elements.

Due to their inability to be effectively cracked by classical computers, RSA, "Diffie-Hellman" (DH), and ECC have long been used for secure key exchange. Quantum computers, on the other hand, use qubits to operate and are capable of solving complicated issues that are unsolvable for conventional systems. By factoring big numbers, Shor's technique demonstrates how sufficiently powerful quantum computers could crack public-key encryption, endangering RSA and related schemes. Additionally, by accelerating brute-force assaults, Grover's technique undermines symmetric encryption like AES meaning future cryptography must evolve to remain secure against quantum threats.

More complex encryption methods that are resistant to quantum attacks are now necessary due to the development of quantum computers. To protect data and preserve anonymity, research is being done on post-quantum cryptography, quantum-resilient cryptographic algorithms, and quantum key distribution systems.

Post-Quantum Cryptography

"Post-Quantum Cryptography" (PQC) consists of cryptographic methods that are resistant to quantum computer assaults. These methods provide secure alternatives to traditional cryptography systems such as "Elliptic Curve Cryptography" (ECC), "Diffie-Hellman" (DH), and "Rivest–Shamir–Adleman" (RSA).

Quantum-Resistant Encryption Techniques (NEW)

Various quantum-resilient approaches can be applied to overcome the future privacy issues:

- **Lattice cryptography:** This method is based on the complicated mathematics of lattice structures. They are not easy to compute even by using classical or quantum machines.

Lattice cryptography can be considered as one of the best solutions for post-quantum encryption due to its robust security and performance.

- **Hash cryptography**: It involves the use of cryptographic hash functions that produce unique digital signatures. They help to ensure integrity and authenticity while providing effective protection against forgery and quantum attacks.
- **Code-based cryptography:** The encryption process is protected by utilizing error-correcting codes. They are designed to prevent any unauthorized access. Moreover, this approach has been proved to be secure and efficient in the long term.
- **Multivariate cryptography:** It is associated with solving multivariable polynomial equation systems, which is a computationally difficult task. As a result, digital signatures and authentication are its main uses.

Quantum Key Distribution (NEW)

"Quantum Key Distribution" (QKD) improves communication security and privacy by securely exchanging encryption keys and detecting eavesdropping attempts using the principles of quantum physics. The following cryptographic techniques: code-based cryptography, hash cryptography, and lattice cryptography, and multivariate cryptography offer enhanced security against potential threats from quantum computing technologies. Moreover, Quantum Key Distribution provides increased communication security by facilitating secure exchange of encryption keys.

7.2. ETHICAL CHALLENGES IN HEALTHCARE AI

Discover important ethical considerations associated with AI in healthcare like bias, privacy, and accountability. Artificial intelligence (AI) is transforming healthcare through better diagnoses, patient-tailored therapies, and streamlined administrative processes. Nevertheless, as AI systems play an increasingly important role in making decisions in medicine, certain ethical issues arise that must be addressed properly. Being aware of them is necessary for everyone involved – healthcare providers, software vendors, policy makers, etc. to make sure AI brings only benefits and does not breach ethics and trust.

This paper examines key ethical dilemmas associated with AI in healthcare – bias, privacy, transparency, and accountability. Provide concrete examples and analyze current regulations in addition to providing recommendations on how to address these problems. As a result, the reader will obtain the full insight into handling ethical considerations in AI-driven healthcare services (Kluge, 2024).

7.2.1. BIAS AND FAIRNESS IN AI HEALTHCARE

In the healthcare sector, the use of AI technology is becoming common when performing diagnosis, developing medical treatment strategies, predicting health issues, and designing customized medicine. With all the benefits AI provides, some ethical concerns such as bias and fairness become significant problems in the application of AI in the healthcare sector.

Bias remains a highly significant ethical issue in AI technology in the healthcare sector. As mentioned earlier, AI technology uses past historical data that may have certain forms of bias within it, resulting from inequalities in society.

According to various studies, some AI technologies that are used for diagnosis have been found to provide accurate results only when applied on majority people, whereas results are not accurate for minorities due to biases in the historical data set.

The ethical challenge involved in AI algorithms when used in health care is that of bias. The problem may affect the objectivity, accuracy, and reliability of decisions made in the medical field. It arises during data collection, labeling, and the development of the algorithm.

- **Sources of Bias in AI Systems**

  There exist different causes of bias, which include but are not limited to biased data acquisition, labeling mistakes, and algorithmic design considerations. For example, when the database is dominated by patients from one particular group, chances are high that the AI will not be able to generalize. Furthermore, people can bring biases into AI by influencing the interpretation and labeling of data.

- **Methods for Mitigating Bias**

  For mitigation, it is critical to consider diverse and balanced databases, incorporate machine learning approaches that account for fairness, and evaluate performance on different subgroups. Collaboration between AI researchers and ethicists would also go a long way towards mitigating bias.

- **Effect of Bias on Healthcare Results**

  The role played by the introduction of bias in artificial intelligence in healthcare will have an effect on the accuracy of disease diagnosis, the recommendations for treatment of the patients, and the priority that is assigned to certain patients.

- **Fairness and Ethics Point**

  In order to ensure that there is fairness in AI-assisted healthcare, it is necessary to create equality in ensuring that all patients get similar results despite their ages, genders, races, or socio-economic classes. In AI development and implementation, ethics mean transparency and inclusiveness.

  There are various ways of eliminating bias in AI technology, including data diversification, fairness-aware algorithms, constant monitoring, and consulting experts. In fairness and ethics when developing AI, patients will benefit from similar results in healthcare irrespective of their socio-economic or personal characteristics.

7.2.2. PRIVACY AND DATA SECURITY CONCERNS

The functioning of artificial intelligence-based healthcare systems depends to a great extent on large amounts of data used to diagnose, develop treatment plans, foresee diseases, and deliver personalized care. However, the use of sensitive patient information raises a number of concerns related to privacy and security issues; therefore, it is essential that this data be protected ethically.

AI-driven healthcare solutions utilize vast amounts of patient information, which might have serious repercussions if accessed or used without the patient's permission.

Additionally, there may be a problem with the regulation of the use of AI in medicine, particularly regarding HIPAA in the USA and GDPR in the EU since it is necessary to share the information.

Privacy and security concerns need to be taken into consideration when working with the use of AI in healthcare systems because AI involves the use of considerable amounts of information.

- **Privacy Issues with AI in Healthcare**

  AI-enabled health care systems need large amounts of patient information, which brings about severe risks for the security and privacy of those systems. Breach of accessing, using, or sharing of the information in the AI system can have negative effects on the patients.

  Moreover, the data-sharing in AI systems is very common, which makes it difficult for such systems to conform to some laws like the "Health Insurance Portability and Accountability Act" (HIPAA) and "General Data Protection Regulation" (GDPR).

- **Balancing Data Utility and Privacy**

  AI technologies like federated learning and difference privacy allow AI algorithms to learn from data without revealing the data on a personal level. It is possible to use such techniques to ensure data usability and privacy protection at the same time.

- **Regulation and Compliance**

  The health industry has a wide range of regulations that must be adhered to when using personal data. Keeping abreast of regulations and taking proper cybersecurity measures are important.

- **Healthcare AI Cybersecurity Issues**

  There is a need for measures to protect healthcare AI systems from various cyber risks such as ransomware attacks and data breaches. The use of proper encryption techniques, reliable storage, and constant security surveillance is critical.

  It is essential to take into account all appropriate steps in terms of securing patients' data privacy and making sure that all regulatory requirements regarding compliance are followed to assure the proper use of AI in the healthcare environment.

Privacy and data protection become highly relevant for AI implementation in the sphere of health care, given that personal data of patients should not become subject to any violations in this context.

7.2.3. ACCOUNTABILITY AND LIABILITY IN AI HEALTHCARE

The use of AI technologies in the medical field has improved precision and productivity in both diagnosis and treatments. At the same time, the use of such technologies in the healthcare setting raises ethical and legal challenges that may emerge in case something goes wrong due to the use of such technologies.

Establishing responsibility in case of harm inflicted or malfunctions related to such technologies constitutes an important moral challenge. In this regard, it becomes necessary to establish who is going to be responsible – whether the developers or the health care organizations using the technology. Ethical and legal regulations should be established to provide clarity regarding liability.

- **AI in Healthcare - Issues and Ethical Implications of Accountability**

  These include responsibility, transparency, and good governance when discussing ethics in the sense of accountability that arises in the use of AI technology in medicine, especially when it results in medical blunders.

- **Ethical Issues Concerning Accountability of AI in Medicine**

  There arise ethical considerations when there is harm caused through AI technology applications. The issue of liability and whether it lies with the software company, the practitioner or other parties comes into play.

  The need therefore arises for well-defined policies concerning liability in malpractice cases arising from the use of AI.

- **Current Legal Perspectives**

  At present, responsibility generally lies with the health care providers using AI, although things may change in the future, with AI becoming more independent. The governments of some countries are investigating legal ways to ensure that developers of AI technologies will be held responsible for their performance.

- **Mechanisms for Ensuring Accountability**

  Keeping audit trails, documenting processes involved, validating AI systems, and training clinicians in the use of AI could help improve accountability.

- **Transparency and Explainability of AI**

  Explainability and transparency in AI algorithms help clarify how decisions are made by medical practitioners and help increase their accountability. Explainability helps build trust and makes it easier to spot any faults or individuals responsible for failure.

- **Governance and Ethical Oversight's Importance**

  Hospitals must create governance and ethical oversight committees in order to oversee the integration of artificial intelligence technology, identify possible threats, and ensure adherence to laws and ethical considerations.

The existence of liability guidelines, accountability frameworks, explainable artificial intelligence algorithms, and governance frameworks is crucial in order to use artificial intelligence technology ethically within healthcare institutions. The issues of accountability and liability are expected to remain the most pressing issues in AI health care owing to the large number of stakeholders involved and rapid advancements in artificial intelligence (Jain et al., 2025).

7.3. BIAS, FAIRNESS, AND TRANSPARENCY

Fairness and prejudice in AI are significant issues that have received a lot of attention recently. It is critical to make sure AI systems are impartial, fair, and equitable as they are employed more and more in a variety of fields and applications. This is a thorough explanation of bias and fairness in AI. and AI transparency is knowing what data artificial intelligence systems use, how they make judgements, and why they generate particular outcomes. In a nutshell, AI transparency is like giving people a glimpse into the inner workings of AI, enabling them to comprehend and have faith in these systems (Organization & others, 2021).

7.3.1. BIAS AND FAIRNESS IN AI FOR HEALTH CARE SYSTEMS

The applications of AI in the healthcare sector include diagnosis of illnesses, formulation of treatment strategies, disease prediction, medical imagery, and personalization of medicine. However, the use of AI technology in the healthcare sector poses the risk of biases because biases can be induced from biases in the datasets used to train algorithms, in algorithms themselves, and even in human biases.

Biases in healthcare AI applications pose challenges to diagnosis of illnesses, inappropriate treatment of patients, and patient prioritization. Past experiences, social biases, and data inadequacies could increase bias risks that lead to disparities in the healthcare outcomes of marginalized groups.

Bias can occur at various stages of the AI process including data gathering, development and training of algorithms, and decision making. Biases in AI applications in health care may affect the performance of diagnostic processes through AI technology.

Types of Bias in AI Healthcare

1. **Sampling Bias:** The bias emerges when the training samples do not accurately represent the population at large. The healthcare use cases will suffer from poor model performance because of biased sampling and make healthcare decisions that are not uniform.
2. **Algorithmic Bias:** In this case, there are errors in the design or coding of the AI algorithm, which favors one feature above others and leads to discrimination. In the healthcare context, it will mean that the diagnosis, prediction, and treatment are biased.
3. **Confirmation Bias:** In this scenario, the AI makes decision based on past patterns rather than discovering any new trends. The bias will limit objective decision-making in healthcare.
4. **Measurement Bias:** This form of bias is related to the process of collecting data. For example, the collected data may be skewed in favor of some populations, leading to incorrect analysis and decision making in healthcare applications.

The negative impact of sampling bias, algorithmic bias, confirmation bias, and measurement bias on the performance of AI in the healthcare sector can be achieved through the inaccurate prediction and differential decision-making.

7.3.2. FAIRNESS IN AI HEALTHCARE

Fairness in AI pertains to the attempt to detect, minimize, and ultimately eliminate algorithmic biases to guarantee equality and ethics in terms of equal treatment of all individuals. As far as the use of AI in healthcare is concerned, fairness is important because AI should treat different patients equally and without discrimination. This concept guarantees equality, justice, transparency, and fairness and prevents discrimination in healthcare services.

One can consider various aspects of fairness in healthcare AI. For instance, group fairness involves the equality of AI treatments to various demographic groups and the absence of disproportionate treatment in favour or against certain demographic groups. There exist several measures to assess group fairness like equal opportunity or demographic parity. Personal equity, in turn, implies similar treatment for similar people regardless of their demographic group affiliation.

Procedural fairness involves equality, transparency, and accountability at all stages of AI healthcare process. Counterfactual fairness implies that an algorithmic decision will be identical for patients despite differences in some of their characteristics in hypothetical scenarios. Causal fairness helps reduce the effect of historical inequality by emphasizing causation instead of biased historical correlations. All these factors contribute to fair AI healthcare practices.

The two main concerns in relation to ethics in AI healthcare systems are bias and fairness due to the potential effects that these may have in increasing existing inequalities within the health care system. There is need to address different types of bias and use fairness to achieve an effective health care system for all people.

7.3.3. TRANSPARENCY AND EXPLAINABILITY IN AI HEALTHCARE

Transparency of AI is defined by the extent to which AI systems have been created, skilled, and utilized in making decisions. In the healthcare sector, it becomes important to be transparent since the AI is increasingly being used in diagnoses, disease treatment and prognosis, among other uses. Transparency promotes trust, accountability, fairness, ethics as well as the knowledge of how AI results come about.

Transparency is one of the critical factors associated with AI applications in the health industry as it allows to comprehend the decision-making process of AI systems.

Key Components of AI Transparency in Healthcare

- **Understanding AI Decisions**

  AI transparency ensures that healthcare professionals and stakeholders understand the reasoning behind AI-generated decisions. The transparency in decision making leads to decreased likelihood of bias, promotes ethics, and enhances confidence in clinical advice.

- **Accountability and Responsibility**

  By making AI transparent, one can achieve increased accountability where developers, health care organizations, and other institutions are able to oversee the performance of the AI and take responsibility for mistakes or any undesirable outcomes that happen.

- **Trust and Acceptance**

  Transparency increases the trust on AI technologies by making clinicians and patients understand how AI systems work. In an environment such as healthcare whereby decisions have direct impacts on patient welfare, trust is necessary for AI adoption.

  In general, transparency increases accountability, builds trust, and encourages responsible AI adoption in healthcare. AI systems that are transparent are bound to increase reliability and acceptance of clinicians and patients alike.

Applications of AI Transparency in Healthcare

There are many reasons why AI transparency promotes the moral application of AI in healthcare:

- **Building Trust:** Transparency makes it easier for patients and medical professionals to understand how AI tools are used to use healthcare data.
- **Fairness and Reliability:** Information about algorithms and datasets available to everyone can be used to assess AI fairness and minimize healthcare biases.
- **Accountability:** Through increased visibility, AI transparency promotes monitoring and auditing AI decisions and processes.
- **Regulatory Compliance:** Transparency ensures the regulation compliance concerning healthcare and AI governance practices.

AI transparency is crucial for healthcare because it fosters greater accountability, justice, and trust, and regulation that it brings about. Transparency assists in gaining insights into how decisions have been made through the use of AI technology. It ensures that there are ethical and fair results, efficient auditing, and adherence to all healthcare regulations.

Transparency is extremely necessary in regards to the ethical use of AI in healthcare. It enables the development of increased trust, accountability, and regulatory compliance. This also increases the efficiency of decision making. The problem of complex algorithms and privacy issues can be solved to increase transparency of AI in the healthcare environment.

7.4. POLICY RECOMMENDATIONS AND BEST PRACTICES

AI in healthcare is bringing various benefits such as better clinical decision making, diagnosis, treatment delivery, and management efficiency. Nevertheless, proper implementation of AI technology necessitates an effective governance structure as well as adequate accountability and regulation to avoid misuse and potential threats that come with using AI in the health sector. Thus, AI recommendations need to be provided.

1. **Guidelines for Appropriate AI Use:** AI usage should always be within well-defined clinical scopes of practice. Professionals should make decisions about whether AI is helping, what requires review, and what should be finally decided by humans.
2. **Compliance Standards:** The regulation of AI should be stringent to guarantee safety and ethics but also should give room for flexibility so that AI is accessible to small or poor healthcare facilities.
3. **Accountability and Transparency:** AI technology should be transparent in its decision-making process. It is also important for developers and healthcare organizations to retain accountability of AI technology through auditing.

4. **Accountability and Liability Frameworks:** Responsibility guidelines are necessary to clarify liability issues arising due to harm caused by AI. Because AI outpaces legislation, there is a need to update laws in order to protect patients and provide clarity on liability issues.

5. **Knowing the Limitations of AI:** It is important for users in the field of health care to understand the limitations associated with AI. There needs to be an understanding of bias, errors, correlation vs. causation, among others in order to avoid making medical mistakes.

Good AI governance in health care involves clearly outlined guidelines on how AI is to be used in practice. The guidelines should incorporate balanced regulation, transparency, and accountability principles. There is also a need to establish responsibility guidelines, update legal framework concerning liability issues, and create awareness on AI limitations.

7.4.1. BEST PRACTICES FOR ETHICAL AI IN HEALTHCARE

Deploying AI in an ethical manner in healthcare will necessitate the observance of some best practices aimed at ensuring the proper usage of the technology. The principles in question include upholding human dignity, avoiding bias, accountability, transparency, confidentiality, and regular monitoring of the AI systems deployed.

- Ensure human dignity in AI use
- Reduce bias and ensure fairness
- Maintain accountability and oversight
- Promote transparency in decisions
- Protect patient privacy
- Continuously monitor and validate AI systems

Recommendations on policies and ethical best practices are critical for responsible implementation of AI in healthcare services. There are many approaches that include governance, accountability, transparency, human control and constant evaluation that may help hospitals to derive maximum gains from AI and reduce its associated risks ethically, legally and clinically.

7.4.2. PRIVACY-BY-DESIGN AND DATA GOVERNANCE

The "Privacy-by-Design" (PbD) concept entails integrating privacy features at the earliest stage when designing information systems, technologies, and even business processes. In other words, PbD addresses privacy challenges by prevention rather than reaction, which makes it quite vital in view of increased data gathering practices and users' privacy concerns, including those related to health care and digital technologies.

Apart from being necessary for the adherence to stringent regulations like GDPR, where privacy must be embedded by default, PbD is also considered a strategic advantage as it helps to avoid any breaches, avoid potential fines, and build trust among users. In this regard, the use of PbD becomes an important factor that may positively affect reputation and provide a competitive advantage.

Proactivity, privacy as default, designing for privacy, complete functioning, end-to-end security, transparency, and respect for user privacy are some of these tenets among others. Together, these principles provide the necessary bedrock for proper governance and data management in the contemporary world.

The idea of Privacy by Design is not only important but essential for proper and secure data management in the digital world. Privacy by Design entails designing your organization's information system in a manner that will ensure security right from the beginning, thus minimizing risks and other related issues like legal troubles while at the same time building customer confidence. Privacy by Design goes beyond better data protection to promote transparency and accountability as well.

7.5. FUTURE DIRECTIONS AND RESEARCH OPPORTUNITIES

The rapid pace of innovation in AI in the field of healthcare has brought about a significant change in the decision-making processes, diagnoses, personalization, and healthcare management. However, in addition to all these changes, some important ethical, technical, and legal issues have arisen as well. Future research on AI should consider safety, equity, responsibility, and accountability as well as maximize efficiency and usefulness.

Moreover, increased reliance on AI in conjunction with electronic health records, images, genomics, and wearable devices has led to an increasing amount of complex data that requires analysis and interpretation. Thus, not only do new opportunities appear, but at the same time, a number of problems arise in relation to such aspects as data accuracy, compatibility, and patients' privacy issues. As AI gets more autonomous and widely used in clinical practice, its reliability and ethicality acquire particular importance.

So, the future directions in this field include the development of safe and responsible AI solutions for the healthcare sector.

7.5.1. FUTURE DIRECTIONS IN AI HEALTHCARE

The future of AI in healthcare should include the development of intelligent systems that can perform better in terms of safety, transparency, and reliability in clinical settings. With continued growth in AI technology, the use of AI in diagnosis, treatment, and health management among others is anticipated to increase tremendously. However, along with this will come the ethical concerns regarding data security, data privacy, bias, and regulation. The main aim for future research in AI health care should include developing intelligent and responsible AI technology for the benefit of healthcare(Chaudhuri & Ghosh, 2025).

Trustworthy and explainable AI is another important future direction for the research and development of AI in the healthcare sector. Since most of the healthcare AI models operate as "black boxes," the interpretability of their outputs becomes crucial for establishing clinical trust and making informed decisions. XAI studies are intended to promote transparency of AI outputs.

Privacy-preserving AI techniques will remain relevant to ensure security of processing patient's sensitive information while retaining the necessary model accuracy. Federated learning, differential privacy approaches, and synthetic data generation will become increasingly popular.

Future studies will focus on advancing impartial and equitable healthcare AI solutions. The development of diverse datasets, fairness-aware machine learning algorithms, and continuous monitoring of algorithmic biases will be the priorities to create an equitable healthcare system. In addition, human-AI interaction models will remain highly topical for further improvement of existing AI tools. Human-in-the-loop approach will help clinicians retain full responsibility for making medical decisions with AI supporting their efforts.

The future of AI for the healthcare sector will be determined by the development of explainable AI technology, trustworthy AI, privacy-enhancing AI, and human-in-the-loop systems among others. This move seeks to tackle the current challenges of non-explainability, data privacy issues, algorithmic biases and more. With the implementation of concepts such as XAI, federated learning, and human-in-the-loop among others, AI for healthcare in the future is expected to be more reliable and ethical as well as more clinically focused and patient-oriented.

7.5.2. RESEARCH OPPORTUNITIES IN AI HEALTHCARE

AI opportunities for improving healthcare have been rapidly evolving due to increased utilization of intelligent systems for diagnosing diseases and treatment. On one hand, there are numerous advancements in the area, facilitated by large datasets available within healthcare. On the other hand, there have emerged many challenges such as the privacy concerns and reliability of the technologies used.

Several research opportunities in this sector are emerging. Among them is the formulation of robust ethics-based and AI governance structures that will regulate AI application in healthcare, taking into account both patient safety and legal requirements.

Additionally, there is room for further AI security and risks mitigation studies with regard to how healthcare facilities can be protected against cyber threats, adversarial attacks, and breaches in data security. There is growing research in AI and personalized medicine whereby AI uses genetic, clinical, and lifestyle data to create tailor-made solutions for individuals.

Another promising opportunity is the use of synthetic data in healthcare AI training in order to enhance AI effectiveness without compromising patient data or dependence on real-world data. Lastly, scalable and globally accessible AI applications will also receive considerable research attention in the future.

The future for artificial intelligence technology in healthcare involves developing a system that is ethical, transparent, safe, and unbiased. Future developments in technologies such as explainable AI, privacy protection, bias elimination, and human and AI interaction will be very important in the creation of future generations of healthcare systems. The result will be a system that is efficient in addition to being safe for patients.

7.5.3. TRUSTWORTHY, ROBUST, AND EXPLAINABLE HEALTHCARE AI

Explanation and reliability are two important features for making use of AI-based applications safely in health care. Clinical decision-making is about making choices that affect lives directly. Therefore, the AI application used for clinical decision-making needs to be explainable, reliable, and trustworthy.

Key Features of Reliable Healthcare AI

Reliable, secure, and interpretable AI is crucial in ensuring the safe and efficient implementation of artificial intelligence within medicine. The field involves creating technologies that are transparent, secure, reliable, and ethically/clinically sound, thus fostering evidence-based medicine practice.

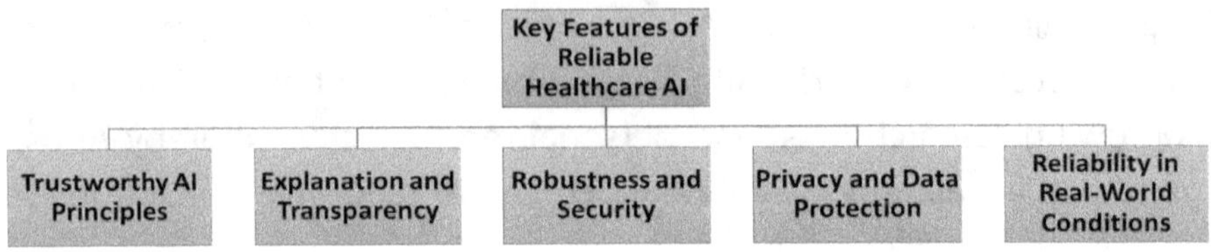

Figure 7.1: Key Features of Reliable Healthcare

Source: Author (2026)

The figure shows Reliable Healthcare AI Framework, which is made up of five major components: Trustworthy AI Principles, Explanation & Transparency, Robustness & Security, Privacy & Data Protection, and Reliability in Reality. This concept is important in making sure that the application of AI technology in the healthcare field is safe and ethical.

1. **Trustworthy AI Principles:** AI technology relies on principles such as ethical considerations, fairness, explainability, security, transparency, and human-centered value. Such features guarantee reliability of AI systems when applied to healthcare.

2. **Explanation and Transparency:** Explainable artificial intelligence (XAI) enables clinicians to understand AI's reasoning process used for prediction. The feature reduces the "black box" effect and increases the level of decision-making confidence (Kose et al., 2024).

3. **Robustness and Security:** Reliable AI solutions should be protected against adversarial attacks, privacy violation, and manipulated data input. Besides, robust models tolerate noisy information efficiently.

4. **Privacy and Data Protection:** The AI technology should ensure that private and confidential data remains unextracted

or misused by any third party. Secure learning techniques can be used in this regard.

5. **Reliability in Real-World Conditions:** The reliability of AI technology depends on its ability to produce consistent results even in different conditions of data availability and imperfections of data distribution.

Trustworthy healthcare AI can be assured by ethical principles, fair AI design, explainability of decisions made, robustness against attacks, privacy of data, and performance in real environments. Taken together, these features guarantee that AI-based technologies become reliable and usable for clinical purposes.

Safe application of AI technology requires an intelligent system to be trustworthy, robust, and understandable. Transparency, security, fairness, and reliability play an important role here in building clinical confidence and making ethical decisions. They make the integration of intelligent systems into the health care system effective.

7.6. CHAPTER SUMMARY

This chapter opens with an overview of emerging technologies in privacy-enhancing AI, namely homomorphic encryption, synthetic data generation, and quantum-safe cryptography. The first one makes it possible to conduct computations in the encrypted form to ensure the safety of patient information during processing. Synthetic data generation helps develop and train models in health care institutions without any use of actual patients' information, thus minimizing possible breaches of privacy and providing data security. Finally, quantum-safe cryptography is described as the solution to prevent potential attacks of future quantum computers, which can break the conventional cryptography systems used in healthcare institutions now.

Ethical concerns related to healthcare AI are subsequently considered in greater detail, with an emphasis on such problems as bias, privacy, and accountability. The usage of training data in machine learning processes is associated with possible amplification or reproduction of implicit biases which can result in inequality of treatment outcomes among different patient populations. Privacy concerns are also relevant to artificial intelligence as large amounts of private information are used, thus increasing the risk of data breaches and other threats related to sensitive data. In addition, it is extremely challenging to identify who is responsible when an AI system makes mistakes and generates harmful results.

Bias, fairness, and transparency are extensively discussed in this chapter. Biases may emerge from biased data collection, flawed algorithms, or faulty measurements that influence diagnostic and therapeutic processes adversely. On the contrary, when it comes to the fundamental fairness in AI, this refers to ensuring equal quality of care to be provided to the patient regardless of his/her demographic or social-economic background; whereas, transparency and explainability give the opportunity to gain deeper insights into the decision-making process.

Recommendations on policy and good practice are also mentioned in the reading; namely, there is an emphasis on having a proper governance structure, human oversight, transparency, and monitoring put in place. One of the approaches that should be taken into account here is the approach known as Privacy by Design; namely, this means that privacy should be incorporated in the very process of developing these AI technologies, thereby improving their regulatory compliance and decreasing any risks that may occur.

In conclusion, one may note that the role of the trustworthy, reliable, and explainable health care AI systems should be noted. The discussed AI systems need to be reliable and safe enough to function effectively in clinical environments and maintain privacy and safety of the protected patient-related information. Speaking about the general idea of this chapter, it may be said that the important contribution of AI technologies into the health care sphere was considered here. It is, however, possible only when all ethical issues are taken into account.

Multiple Choice Questions (MCQs)

1. **Which of the following is a key goal of privacy-preserving AI?**
    A. Increasing model complexity
    B. Protecting user data while enabling analysis
    C. Reducing computational cost
    D. Eliminating the need for datasets
2. **Which technology helps train AI models without sharing raw data?**
    A. Blockchain
    B. Federated Learning
    C. Cloud Computing
    D. Data Mining
3. **Differential privacy is primarily used to:**
    A. Speed up AI models
    B. Encrypt hardware
    C. Add noise to data to protect individual privacy
    D. Improve data visualization
4. **What is a major ethical concern in healthcare AI?**
    A. High electricity consumption
    B. Lack of internet access
    C. Misdiagnosis due to biased algorithms
    D. Overuse of hardware

5. **Bias in AI systems often originates from:**
   - A. Hardware limitations
   - B. Training data
   - C. User interfaces
   - D. Network speed
6. **Which concept ensures AI decisions can be understood by humans?**
   - A. Scalability
   - B. Transparency
   - C. Automation
   - D. Compression
7. **Fairness in AI aims to:**
   - A. Maximize profit
   - B. Reduce computation time
   - C. Ensure equal treatment across different groups
   - D. Increase data size
8. **Which of the following is a recommended best practice for ethical AI?**
   - A. Ignoring regulations
   - B. Using only large datasets
   - C. Regular auditing of AI systems
   - D. Limiting user interaction
9. **What role do policies play in AI development?**
   - A. Increase coding speed
   - B. Ensure responsible and ethical use
   - C. Reduce hardware cost
   - D. Replace developers

10. **Future research in AI ethics is likely to focus on:**
    A. Reducing internet usage
    B. Improving gaming systems
    C. Enhancing accountability and fairness
    D. Eliminating AI systems

Answers

1	2	3	4	5	6	7	8	9	10
B	B	C	C	B	B	C	C	B	C

BIBLIOGRAPHY

AbuRumman, S. A. (2026). *The HIPAA Compliance Blueprint: A Complete Guideline for Healthcare Providers, Practices, and Business Associates*. CRC Press.

Anandan, R., Pal, S., Balaganesh, D., & Badie, F. (2026). *Federated Learning for Healthcare: Applications with Case Studies*. CRC Press.

Catt, H. J. (2018). *Cost-effectiveness modelling for benefit-risk assessment*. The University of Liverpool (United Kingdom).

Chaudhuri, T., & Ghosh, J. (2025). *Future Trends in Artificial Intelligence for Medical Applications* (pp. 509–570). https://doi.org/10.4018/979-8-3693-9816-6.ch020

Cheng, Z. (2022). *Differential Privacy in Multi-agent Reinforcement Learning*. University of Technology Sydney (Australia).

Chorghade, M. S. (2006). *Drug discovery and development, volume 1: drug discovery* (Vol. 1). John Wiley \& Sons.

Chow, S.-C., & Liu, J.-P. (2004). *Design and analysis of clinical trials: concepts and methodologies* (Vol. 2). Wiley Online Library.

Data, M. I. T. C., & others. (2016). *Secondary analysis of electronic health records* (Vol. 183). Springer.

Davidoff, S. (2019). *Data breaches: crisis and opportunity*. Addison-Wesley Professional.

Eappen, P., Vajjhala, N. R., Zikos, D., & Davidson, K. P. (2025). *Remote Monitoring and Wearable Devices in Healthcare*. Springer.

El Emam, K. (2013). *Guide to the de-identification of personal health information*. CRC Press.

Goldreich, O. (2001). *Foundations of cryptography: volume 2, basic applications* (Vol. 2). Cambridge university press.

Guo, S., Han, L., & Guo, Y. (2024). *Advanced Technologies in Healthcare*. Springer.

Hassan, A., Prasad, V. K., Bhattacharya, P., Dutta, P., & Damaševičius, R. (2023). *Federated learning and AI for healthcare 5.0*. IGI Global.

Hoffmann, C. H., Hoffmann, C. H., & Berg. (2017). *Assessing Risk Assessment*. Springer.

Imoize, A. L., Balas, V. E., Solanki, V. K., Lee, C.-C., & Obaidat, M. S. (2023). *Handbook of Security and Privacy of AI-Enabled Healthcare Systems and Internet of Medical Things*. CRC press Boca Raton, FL, USA:

Iniewski, K. (2009). *Medical imaging: principles, detectors, and electronics*. John Wiley \& Sons.

Jain, M., (Sanja), M. J., & Sinha, S. (2025). *AI Adoption in Healthcare Industry 4.0*. Springer.

Kayem, A. V. D. M., Akl, S. G., & Martin, P. (2010). *Adaptive cryptographic access control* (Vol. 48). Springer Science \& Business Media.

Kim, K., & Tanuwidjaja, H. C. (2021). *Privacy-preserving deep learning: a comprehensive survey*. Springer.

Kluge, E.-H. W. (2024). *The Ethics of Artificial Intelligence in Healthcare: From Hands-on Practice to Policy-making*. Springer Nature.

Kose, U., Sengoz, N., Chen, X., & Saucedo, J. A. M. (2024). *Explainable artificial intelligence (XAI) in healthcare*. CRC Press.

Le Ny, J. (2020). *Differential Privacy for Dynamic Data*. Springer.

Li, J. J., & Corey, E. J. (2013). *Drug discovery: practices, processes, and perspectives*. John Wiley \& Sons.

Lilhore, U. K., Simaiya, S., Poongodi, M., & Dutt, V. (2024). *Federated learning and privacy-preserving in healthcare AI*. IGI Global.

Liu, H. H. (2011). *Software performance and scalability: a quantitative approach*. John Wiley \& Sons.

Mishra, A. (2024). *Scalable AI and Design Patterns Design, Develop, and Deploy Scalable AI Solutions*.

Ng, R. (2015). *Drugs: from discovery to approval*. John Wiley \& Sons.

Nordlinger, B., Villani, C., & Rus, D. (2020). *Healthcare and artificial intelligence*. Springer.

Organization, W. H., & others. (2021). *Ethics and governance of artificial intelligence for health: WHO guidance*. World Health Organization.

Ouaissa, M., & Ouaissa, M. (2024). *Offensive and Defensive Cyber Security Strategies: Fundamentals, Theory and Practices*. CRC Press.

Panagoulias, D. P., Tsihrintzis, G. A., & Virvou, M. (2025). *Artificial Intelligence-Empowered Bio-medical Applications: Challenges, Solutions and Development Guidelines* (Vol. 49). Springer Nature.

Patil, V. A., Bojarajulu, B., Mittal, A., & Padhi, D. K. (2026). *A Comprehensive Guide on Role of AI in Healthcare*. Shashwat Publication.

Pelikan, M., Sastry, K., & Cantú-Paz, E. (2006). *Scalable optimization via probabilistic modeling: From algorithms to applications* (Vol. 33). Springer Science \& Business Media.

Pereira, N. A. (2025). *Medication Safety Following Electronic Health Record Implementation in Pediatric Intensive Care*. Queen's University (Canada).

Pezoulas, V., Exarchos, T., & Fotiadis, D. (2020). Medical data sharing, harmonization and analytics. In *Medical Data Sharing, Harmonization and Analytics*. https://doi.org/10.1016/c2018-0-00523-x

Pratap, A., Patel, Y. S., Yadav, R. N., Ahmadian, A., & Yadav, A. K. (2025). *AI-Driven Smart Healthcare: Powered by Hyperscale Computing and Next Generation Networks*. John Wiley \& Sons.

Rahaman, M., Arya, V., Orozco, S. M., & Pappachan, P. (2024). Secure multi-party computation (SMPC) protocols and privacy. In *Innovations in Modern Cryptography* (pp. 193–218). IGI Global Scientific Publishing.

Raza, A. (2023). *Secure and privacy-preserving federated learning with explainable artificial intelligence for smart healthcare system*. University of Kent (United Kingdom).

Sahai, A. (2013). *Secure multi-party computation*. SAGE Publications Limited.

Salomon, D. (2012). *Data privacy and security*. Springer Science \& Business Media.

Sharma, S. (2019). *Data privacy and GDPR handbook*. John Wiley \& Sons.

Singh, A. K., & Kumar, S. (2024). *Security, Privacy, and Trust in WBANs and E-Healthcare*. CRC Press.

Sinha, P. K., Sunder, G., Bendale, P., Mantri, M., & Dande, A. (2012). *Electronic health record: standards, coding systems, frameworks, and infrastructures*. John Wiley \& Sons.

Weber, R. H., & Heinrich, U. I. (2012). *Anonymization*. Springer Science \& Business Media.

Weske, M., Vossen, G., & Medeiros, C. B. (1996). *Scientific workflow management: WASA architecture and applications*. Universität Münster. Angewandte Mathematik und Informatik.

Xhafa, F. (2024). *Federated Learning for Digital Healthcare Systems*. Elsevier.

ABOUT THE AUTHORS

Ajit Sahu is a Director of Engineering and AI Architect with deep expertise in privacy engineering, AI governance, enterprise digital transformation, and scalable frontend architecture. He has led major technology initiatives across retail, healthcare, finance, and privacy-compliance domains, including AI-powered consent management, cookie classification, data protection automation, and secure customer-facing platforms. Ajit is also active in thought leadership, research, and industry innovation, with a focus on building responsible, privacy-preserving AI systems for regulated enterprises.

Sanjoy Mukherjee is an Associate Director with over two decades of experience designing and leading enterprise Life Sciences CRM platforms. His expertise spans Veeva Vault CRM, Salesforce Life Sciences Cloud, IQVIA OCE, and MuleSoft, and he has shaped next-generation CRM strategies for many of the world's leading pharmaceutical companies across North America and Europe.

An inventor and researcher at the intersection of artificial intelligence and life sciences, Sanjoy holds a granted German utility patent and a pending US patent for AI-driven CRM systems. His peer-reviewed research has appeared in IEEE conferences and JMIR journals, covering deep learning for medical imaging, biomedical signal classification, and machine learning for public health surveillance. He serves as a peer reviewer for IEEE and other international conferences and has applied for IEEE Senior Member status.

Sanjoy holds a B.Tech in Electrical Engineering and is completing a Postgraduate Program in Artificial Intelligence and Machine Learning at the University of Texas at Austin. He is Salesforce and Veeva certified and a PRINCE2 Practitioner. He lives in Bridgewater, New Jersey, with his family.

www.ingramcontent.com/pod-product-compliance
Lightning Source LLC
LaVergne TN
LVHW022206200926
848481LV00006B/1860
* 9 7 9 8 9 0 5 6 0 3 5 1 8 *